Educating and entertaining your children online with Carol Vorderman

When we were children, we didn't even know of computers, let alone imagine a system where all of them might be connected up to a global network allowing us to communicate with each other directly and search for information which no single library could ever hope to hold.

But that is the world our children are growing up in and the internet is the most powerful tool they will have to use. The net can be a wonderful, exciting, educational, entertaining place to be and children take to it very simply. We've all experienced the moment when our children explain to us how to use a new piece of technology, whether it's the video recorder, camera, mobile phone messaging system, or a computer scanner. Well, this book hopes to redress some of the balance. We hope that if you are one of the army of parents who feel that they know less than their children about the internet, then this will be a great start.

In it, we tell you everything you need to know about the education system in the UK and how to find out about it online. We give you a comprehensive list of sites which have marvellous databases of research for school projects and also sites for leisure, for pets, sports and parties. This book is an action book giving you lots of information which you can use directly: and for those who don't know their CD ROMs from their MP3, then a full glossary of terms will help you. We are also concerned that you watch over your children so that they learn to use the net in a safe environment. Please be vigilant. Remember that at the moment, just as your child has a gateway into a new world, that same world can force its way into your child's life whether they want it or not. And that happens in the form of junk mail (most of it sexually explicit) or advertising which as yet is largely unregulated. Don't let this spoil the internet for you. Let it become a part of your life and you'll see just how much you can learn from being a switched online parent. Enjoy it, but be safe.

Carol Vorderman

Educating and Entertaining Your Children Online

with *Carol Vorderman*

www.parents.org.uk
The Web Site for parents by parents

Prentice
Hall

An imprint of **Pearson Education**

London · New York · Toronto · Sydney · Tokyo · Singapore
Madrid · Mexico City · Munich · Paris

Pearson Education Limited
Head Office:
Edinburgh Gate
Harlow CM20 2JE
Tel: +44 (0)1279 623623
Fax: +44 (0)1279 431059

London Office:
128 Long Acre
London WC2E 9AN
Tel: +44 (0)20 7447 2000
Fax: +44 (0)20 7240 5771

First published in Great Britain in 2001

ISBN 0–130–28645–1

British Library Cataloguing-in-Publication Data
A catalogue record for this book is available from the British Library.

10 9 8 7 6 5 4 3 2 1

Inside photograph by Tino Tedaldi.
Typeset by Pantek Arts Ltd, Maidstone, Kent.
Printed and bound by Biddles of Guildford and King's Lynn.

The Publisher's policy is to use paper manufactured from sustainable forests.

Contents

● ● ● ● ● ●

Part 1 Introduction
● ● ● ● ● ● ● ● ● ● ● ● ●

Part 2 Education
● ● ● ● ● ● ● ● ● ● ● ● ●

Part 3 Leisure and health

Foreword

● ● ● ● ● ● ●

Welcome to Parents Online. Please don't let our name fool you – we're here to provide information and inspiration for anyone who cares for children, not just parents. You'll find lots of information and inspiration in this book and on our site on the world wide web (**www.parents.org.uk**).

Parents Online was established in the summer of 1999 by a group of parents who, as is often the case, met through their children. Although several of us are actively involved in the internet industry, as UK parents we felt frustrated by what we found on the web. We all had our own experiences of good sites, but there appeared to be no consensus and focal point for us parents.

Parents Online aims to provide a web community for UK parents of pre-secondary school age children (2–12 years), although of course other nations are not excluded. The site provides comprehensive information and advice on the key parenting areas: education, health and leisure. Full use is made of internet technology, allowing parents to air their views, vote on topical debates, and even sell their old toys through the free ads.

Just as Parents Online has fulfilled a recognised need for an UK site for parents, this book aims to provide a comprehensive guide to parenting and show how the internet can help. In a similar manner this book covers education, health and leisure. Recognising that many parents will be new to the web, there is also an introductory guide to the internet and advice on safe surfing.

This book balances practical advice on being a parent with reviews of some of our favourite websites. On the CD you will find a searchable database of these and other reviews, with direct access to each of the sites – so avoiding the need to type in lengthy web addresses (URLs). To keep up with the ever growing number of new sites, the CD also has an update facility to download the latest set of reviews from Parents Online.

 The text also includes suggestions of activities you can do with your child – look out for the activity icon throughout the book.

If you are a parent, grandparent, carer or simply interested in parenting issues, this book will be an invaluable guide and show how the internet can help.

Simon Lovesey
www.parents.org.uk

Acknowledgements

Although someone's name had to go on the front cover, it is important to recognise the effort that everyone at Parents Online has put into the production of this book. We should mention especially Liz Holliday, who has been one of the major contributors to both the site and the book.

Web reviews

● ● ● ● ● ● ● ● ●

This book contains a selection of some of our favourite websites that we have found useful as parents. Although these were accurate at the time of going to press, by its very nature the internet is evolving so fast that by the time you read this there may be some inaccuracies and omissions. If you wish to submit a site for future consideration or notify us of any changes, please use the web form **www.parents. org.uk/sitesreg.htm**

The CD that accompanies this book includes a database of the web reviews, including many more reproduced within the book. Reviews can be searched by subject and/or key word, then clicking on a web address will take you straight to that web site (assuming an internet connection is present). The database also has a facility to update itself by downloading the latest sets of reviews. Also included is a range of games and colouring pictures.

The CD will start automatically when you insert it into your CD drive. The CD also has an updating facility, allowing the latest version of the database to be downloaded.

Part 1 Introduction

• Introducing the internet

CHAPTER 1

Introducing the internet

● ● ● ● ● ● ● ● ● ● ● ● ● ● ● ● ● ●

Although still in its infancy, the internet is already playing a major role in everyday life. Even if you are just starting out on the net, many of the organisations that you come into contact with will be using the internet in their day-to-day business.

WHAT IS THE INTERNET?

In simple terms the internet is a network of millions of computers based all over the world. These computers are able to share information and resources. Probably one of the most significant factors behind the dramatic growth of the internet is its openness. Regardless of where you are in the world you will be able to use the internet, as long as you can access a telephone service. There is a well defined methodology for individuals and organisations wishing to use the internet to share information.

The internet can be used for a wide range of activities. The most commonly used parts of the internet are:

- **World wide web** (or simply the web) – here you can view and interact with websites. Basic websites allow you to view text and images; more advanced sites also use video, animations and sound. As all the computers are connected together you start to get the benefit of linking, allowing you to easily move from site to site –

surfing the web. With the onset of e-commerce you can also order products online and track the progress of their delivery. The best way to learn about the web is to play with it – this book contains the addresses of plenty of websites to get you started.

- **Newsgroups** – message boards where you can leave messages on subjects that interest you. Naturally, you can also reply to messages left by other people. They are generally text only (though some allow pictures to be posted). Newsgroups are a great way of voicing your views or sharing experiences, and of course making contact with similarly-minded people around the world.
- **E-mail** – a way of sending letters (and documents of various kinds) to people electronically. Very occasionally it can be a bit slow, but generally it's still so fast that on the internet the slang for the ordinary postal service is 'snail mail'. E-mail allows us to keep in touch with friends and family from around the world, usually for the cost of a local phone call.

One of the best things about the internet is that it is there for you whenever you want it – 24 hours a day, seven days a week.

Understanding internet addresses

The internet is vast – computers all over the world are connected to it. That means that an addressing system is needed to ensure that the correct data reaches the correct computer.

Internet addresses are a bit like post-codes. Every computer on the internet has a unique IP (Internet Protocol) address consisting of four sets of numbers, for example 209.207.222.104. This address is used to identify which computer to send information to – whether it's an e-mail message, the contents of a web page, or the messages posted on a newsgroup.

Of course, IP addresses are not very friendly, and they are hard to remember. This is where domain names come in. **www.parents. org.uk** is the domain name for Parents Online. As you can see, it is much easier to use than the raw IP address. A Domain Name Server (DNS) then translates the domain name to its appropriate IP address.

The final sections of the domain name may give you clues to who is behind that particular website, and also its location. For example,

.org.uk indicates a UK-based organisation, **.co.uk** a UK company. A **.com** suffix is probably the most famous. It used to indicate an American-based company, but now it is used around the world.

WHAT DO YOU NEED?

To use any of the parts of the internet, you'll need several things – a computer with a modem (the device that sends and receives messages down the phone line), an account with an Internet Service Provider (ISP, which will allow you to hook into the internet), and the right kind of software. If you are buying a new computer, many now come ready-equipped for the internet.

ISPs

Choosing an ISP can be quite tricky. Some charge a flat monthly fee for unlimited access; others charge per hour; and some don't charge anything, but make money in other ways, such as by putting adverts on the bottom of the messages you send, or charging a high per-minute rate for calls to their helpline (so heaven help you if you get stuck). Increasingly there is a move to include also the cost of the actual phone calls within the overall package. The best advice is to shop around – though do make sure that whoever you choose is available through a local call number (and, if you expect to need internet access when you travel, that they have local numbers all over the country or world).

At the back of this book you will find details of UK Online, a leading ISP.

Usually your ISP will give you the software you need, though if you use a PC some of it may come with Windows. You'll need a browser to look at web pages – the most common are Internet Explorer and Netscape, though there are others. You can look at newsgroups with a web browser, but it means staying online (and probably running up your phone bill) while you do it. Many people prefer to use a dedicated newsreader – if you are using a PC and your ISP hasn't provided you with one, you can download a free copy of Forté Free Agent from **www.forteinc.com**

It's pretty much the same story with e-mail – you can use your web browser, or Outlook Express (provided free with recent versions of Windows), or search the web for other solutions.

Your phone bill

The fear of running up a massive phone bill is of real concern to many people when using the internet. With some planning you can keep your online costs to reasonable levels. When you consider what is available, the internet can offer tremendous value for money. Most ISPs use an 0845 number for access. This is charged at local rates, with the cheapest being at the weekend when you will typically pay 1p per minute. With British Telecom (and some other providers) you can nominate your favourite numbers and receive a discount on call charges, so make your ISP your number-one friend under this scheme.

It is possible to configure your internet connection settings to disconnect the telephone line after a pre-determined period of inactivity. This can usually be accessed from the control panel. However, BT has a minimum charge of 5p per call, so constant connecting and re-connecting may actually cost more.

There is a growing move to offer unmetered internet calls. A fixed monthly fee includes the cost of phone calls and you can then use the internet as much as you wish. In the USA unmetered calls have been credited as one of the key reasons for the rapid adoption of the internet there. At the time of writing the market is in a state of flux, so do shop around.

HOW TO MAKE THE MOST OF THE INTERNET

Browsing

It is very easy to surf from site to site, quickly forgetting where you have been. The 'History' button on your browser will help you track the sites you have previously visited. If you visit a site that you particularly like, save it as a 'Favorite'. If your list of 'Favorites' grows too vast and becomes unmanageable, you can group sites into subject folders.

Increasingly sites are making use of plug-ins – these are extra pieces of software to provide additional functionality. Two of the most popular are RealPlayer (**www.real.com**) for streaming video/audio and Shockwave (**www.shockwave.com**) for interaction/animations.

Search engines

With so many sites, it can be tricky to find the pages on the web that you want. The first thing you'll need to find is a good search engine – that's a website that specialises in finding other websites for you. Some good ones are:

- **www.google.com**
- **www.altavista.co.uk**
- **www.yahoo.co.uk**
- **www.excite.co.uk**
- **www.ask.co.uk**

These will point you in the right direction, although with the ever-growing number of sites do not expect instant results from searching. Often the search engines will lead you to other more specialist sites, which may then link to specific pages that answer your need. Gateway or portal sites that specialise in particular areas are starting to prove very popular. **www.parents.org.uk** is an example of a portal aimed at UK parents.

Content

You'll soon notice that the web has a distinctly American flavour. It's not a great conspiracy – it's just that more Americans have web access than any other nationality.

There's nothing whatever to guarantee the accuracy of any web page you find – so if you're looking for important information, be sure to cross-check it, either off-line or on.

E-mail

One of the most useful e-mail facilities is the ability to respond easily to mail you have received. Clicking on the 'Reply to' button will usually bring up a copy of the mail automatically addressed to its author. You can easily annotate the original message with your comments. Another useful tip is to create your own address book of contacts, avoiding the need to constantly type e-mail addresses – some software will do this for you, automatically adding addresses from mail as it arrives.

Whilst discussing e-mail, a word of warning about viruses. These can be easily distributed via e-mail attachments. Although attachments are very useful for sending files, the best advice is only to open e-mail attachments from known senders. Also make sure that your computer has a current virus checker installed.

Newsgroups

Newsgroups can be a lot of fun, but they also have pitfalls of their own. The main thing to remember is that if you post in one, you are joining a community – and any community has its own rules and has both nice and nasty people. Before you post anything to a newsgroup, take the time to lurk – read without posting – for a while, so that you get the feel of the place. Never post in all capitals – it's hard to read and is considered the equivalent of shouting.

Sooner or later you'll probably get into an argument. These are called flamewars, and can get very acrimonious. Some groups are more prone to them than others. Unless you like being insulted (or insulting people) the best tactic is generally just to walk away – some newsgroup readers allow you to 'killfile' people or subjects. This means your software will stop downloading anything from a particular person or with a specified subject header – and that makes walking away *much* easier!

SAFE SURFING

Although the internet is a marvellous tool, it is still in its infancy and there are many rules for its use which need to be established. So until that time, we must stress that you do everything possible to protect your child while she is online, particularly younger children whose innocence may be destroyed the arrival of sexually explicit junk mail. At the moment, most email addresses allow you access to the world but equally the world has access to you. So be vigilant. One site which does give proper protection from junk mail is **www. privatemail.com**, a new website which requires the sender of an email to know your 'key', a word which must be included in the subject line for that email to be allowed into your mailbox. Try it and see what you think.

The simple rules for safe use are:

- never let your child use an online computer from his own bedroom. Keep the computer in a family room so that you are aware of what is being viewed.
- never let your child give out personal information in a chatroom such as address or telephone number.
- tell your child not to give out personal information to any site without your permission. In America all reputable sites are now forced to ask for parental premission before gaining this information but many other countries still have to agree to these recommendations.
- if your child is engaged in chat rooms, then check yourself to see what is being talked about. In most cases you would be shocked at the amount of explicit and sexual conversation which occurs. Check it first.

Although we hate to have to mention it, a number of paedophiles are now known to use chatrooms regularly as a way of enticing and 'grooming' children online. Their intention is often to eventually meet up with the child to have some sort of sexual encounter. So beware of their techniques which are:

- lying about their age and background. Many will claim to be teenagers (of course, you can claim to be anything online without any checks being made).
- they will encourage your child to talk about her feelings, appearing to be caring and loving individuals.
- they will tell your child that he is special and misunderstood as a way of gaining their trust (what teenager doesn't feel misunderstood?).

- they will eventually ask for private email addresses and telephone numbers as a way of gaining even more assess to your child.
- they will try to gain secrets from your child as a way of driving a wedge of mistrust between you and her.

Many parents have been duped by these techniques assuming that the online relationship was no more than a schoolgirl/boy crush. These are dangerous people and as yet these is little you can do to protect your child against them, apart from continuing to be vigilant and notifying authorities as soon as you suspect something.

Making the internet, and chat in particular, safer for children is an international task and one which takes all sectors – industry, governments, education, police, child-welfare agencies and parents. One organisation called Childnet is active in this area. Go to **www. childnet-int.org** or **www.chatdanger.com**.

There is a variety of technology-based approaches to this problem, involving software tools to block, filter, monitor and manage the content that children can access via the internet. Some of these can be very useful, but, as yet, none of them are infallible, and for many of us they just add further confusion to an already complex technology. Even if we use one or more of these tools on our computers at home, we still have to consider what our children may be exposed to on computers elsewhere.

The starting point, as with any child-safety issue, is to get your child to learn and adopt some basic rules that they carry with them wherever they go. Disney maintains an online site to educate families and children about Safe Surfing, and reinforces the approach by associating the messages with Disney characters.

Disney Safe Surfing **www.disney.co.uk/safesurfing**

From this site you can access a wide variety of information on internet safety. A good way to start is to take the link to the 'Parent's Guide to Safe Surfing'. Here you will find information on the following topics:

- what is the internet?
- what does the internet offer us and our children?
- how is the internet controlled?

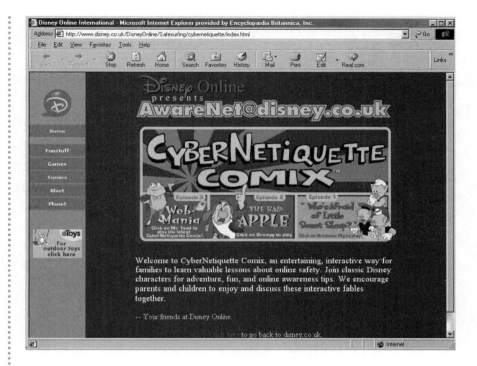

- how to use the internet safely
- online resources to help you use the internet safely.

The online resources section includes most of the following links (we've added a few extra useful ones):

- **Reporting illegal material** – the Internet Watch Foundation is run by the UK internet industry and provides a hotline for people to report material that they think is illegal. Further details can be found at **www.iwf.org.uk/** Illegal material can also be reported to the Inhope Association at **www.inhope.org**
- **Filtering software** – information about various different systems is available at **www.getnetwise.org/tools/** The pros and cons of using internet filtering products are also discussed by the UK Consumer Association Which? at **www.iwf.org.uk/safe/tool.htm**
- **Search engines** – child-safe search engines are listed at **www.safekids.com/search.htm**
- **Safety tips** – further tips for both parents and children are provided by the charity NCH Action for Children on their site at **www.nchafc.org.uk/internet/index.html**

- **Children online** – Childnet International is a UK-based charity concerned with all aspects of children's use of the internet. Find out more at **www.childnet-int.org** Childnet's research for the European Commission looks into the need for internet awareness programmes at **www.netaware.org**
- **Children's resources** – all kinds of tips and ideas to encourage children to get the most from the net are available at **www.launchsite.org**
- **Education** – the government's National Grid for Learning is a useful site for kids, adults, parents and teachers at **www.ngfl.gov.uk** European Schoolnet contains links to various European governments' educational websites at **www.en.eun.org**
- **Glossary** – a useful explanation of internet terms can be found at **www.americalinksup.org/planyourown/intterms.html**
- **International internet rating system** – see the Internet Content Rating Alliance at **www.icra.org**
- **Industry self-regulation** – The Bertelsmann Foundation's report offers information on self-regulation of the internet at **www.stiftung.bertelsmann.de/internetcontent/english/frameset_ home.htm**

The Disney Safe Surfing site provides lots of ways of helping you get the safety message across to your children. For example you could read through and discuss 'Doug's Safe Surfing Tips' together.

Playing on their own, or with you, the children can take the link to 'Patti's CyberNetiquette Comix' at: **www.disney.co.uk/Safesurfing/cybernetiquette/index.html** to view interactive comic stories-with-a-message involving Disney characters such as Mickey Mouse, the Seven Dwarves and the Three Little Pigs.

For those wanting to learn more about what the various content filtering, blocking, monitoring and managing tools actually do, and also links to sites where you can download trial versions and buy the tools, Disney gives the following link: **www.getnetwise.org/tools**

There are a large and growing number of these tools. You can see reviews of some of them at: **www.go.com/WebDir/Family/Parent_Pages/Internet_issues/Internet_content_filters** which provides reviews of 40 sites providing tools and information. Examples of links to sites that sell tools include:

- **www.netnanny.com**
- **www.cyberpatrol.com**
- **www.mcafee.com**
- **www.microsys.com/plain_hm.htm**

The Disney site also provides lots of fun things for kids to do to keep them coming back to the site and reinforcing the safe-surfing message. The site includes activities such as pictures to print out and colour, interactive, comics, games and wallpaper generators.

ISP services

Some ISPs will offer filtering services from their servers.

Other considerations

Most browsers will allow you to configure their security settings, some even give the option to enter sites you do not want your family to visit. There are independent schemes to rate sites, such as RASCi (**www.icra.org**), and you can usually configure your browser to bene-fit from these. However, by the very nature of the magnitude and growth of the internet, such schemes to rate sites can never cover every site and consequently you may find yourself barred from per-fectly acceptable sites.

Using the 'History' function it is possible to see which websites have been visited via your browser. This could be used as a handy check on internet usage and as part of a discussion point within the family. Of course, a knowledgeable child can easily clear the 'History' file, but by making it known and asking why they did this, you may encourage them to think about which sites they visit.

Conclusions

Safe surfing is a serious issue and should be treated seriously. There are plenty of products, services and methods available, but no one solution is likely to deliver the complete answer and devolve parental responsibility. Probably the best advice for parents is to play an active role in their children's internet use and help them develop their own responsibilities.

Part 2 Education

- Schools
- The National Curriculum
- Inspections
- Problems at school
- Getting involved with your child's school
- Helping your child at home

CHAPTER 2

Schools

● ● ● ● ●

Children's education is a major concern for most parents. Discussions on which school children will attend are often made very early. Then there is the emotional pain of the first day and very soon we are into the issues of homework and helping at home. Even at the age of seven, most children will sit official government tests.

This section will help you choose a school, provide background on what happens at school and suggests what you can do to help at home.

CHOOSING A SCHOOL

Choosing your child's school is one of the most important decisions you are ever likely to make.

You may already have made certain decisions, such as whether to send your child to a state or independent school, whether you want your child to go to a church or other religious school, or whether or not you want your child to wear a school uniform. But even if you already know the answers to these questions, you may still find yourself with a choice of schools. Some of these may have a better reputation than others for behaviour or academic excellence; then again, you may feel that your child will simply do better in a certain kind of atmosphere (more creative, say, or more formal).

You may even decide not to send your child to school at all, but to educate them at home instead. The idea may just appeal to you; or if your child has learning or behavioural difficulties, you may feel they will do better at home than in a classroom environment; or you may have realised your child is gifted in some way, and feel that you are more able to help them make the most of their abilities than a teacher.

If you do decide on home schooling, you may find the sections on the National Curriculum (*see* page 29) and activities to do with your child (*see* page 119) particularly useful. The rest of this chapter is about how to choose a school for your child.

Make a game out of investigating the local schools: draw a simple map with your house at the centre; then, using small pieces of paper (or stickers), your child can locate the different schools.

First steps

Start thinking about finding a school for your child when she's about three. Any younger and she, and the schools, may have changed so much by the time she's ready to start that your research has been wasted. Leave it much beyond that and you may not have time to do adequate research, and you may be too late to get your child into your first choice of school.

Department for Education and Employment
http://www.dfee.gov.uk

This large site explains the aims and objectives of the government Department for Education and Employment (DfEE) and how it supports government policy. It explains the structure of the department and responsibilities of the team working in it. There is a wealth of information on education and employment, from the earliest stages of learning through to university and beyond to include life-long learning. Much of the information can be downloaded for printing and photocopying, and various formats are available to match the needs of the user.

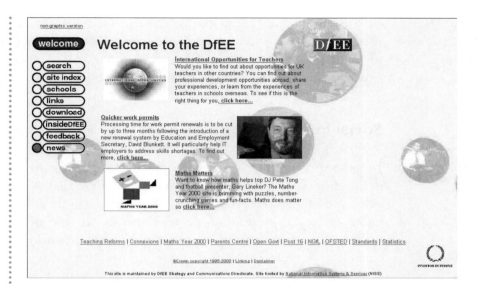

STATE, PRIVATE AND HOME SCHOOLING

Most people have definite ideas about the kind of school they want for their child, but if you haven't yet decided, here are some points to consider.

Costs

State primary schools are of course free, although you may be asked to make a contribution to the parents' association, or help out with fundraising. Independent schools usually charge fees for each term. However, it may be possible to get financial help with these. With home schooling there are no fees as such, but you will need to provide books and a lot of time and expertise, plus perhaps the cost of day trips to museums and so on.

Quality

Some people assume that independent schools give a higher quality of education than state ones. This may not always be the case. You should take into account the catchment areas of the schools and whether the independent schools are selective or not before you jump to conclusions. The quality of home schooling really depends on the expertise and commitment you are able to bring to it.

Social interaction

For some people, part of the point of sending children to an independent school is to provide an environment where they stand the best chance of meeting certain kinds of people; whether this limits or enhances social interaction rather depends on your point of view. Others may welcome the opportunity some state and independent schools give children to meet the widest possible range of people. Home schooling provides a different kind of challenge: you may need to make sure your children socialise enough, but there are local organisations in many areas to help with this.

Home schooling http://homepages.tesco.net/ ~littlebears

This site is intended as a resource for anybody interested in educating their children at home. It is perhaps especially suited to Christians but is intended to be helpful to all. Little Bears Family Homeschool was started by a UK couple who plan to educate their children at home and the site is intended to share their thinking and research with others. The site provides links to support groups in the UK and around the world, information on methods of teaching at home, recommended reading etc.

Formality

Some schools take a much more formal approach than others. This shows itself, for example, in the seating arrangements, the way the children are expected to address their teachers, and the amount of freedom they have to move around in class and organise their own learning. Some children thrive in this formal kind of environment – it helps them concentrate on learning and encourages them to develop self-discipline. Timid children sometimes do very well in more formal situations. However, it doesn't suit everyone. Many children work better in a more laid-back atmosphere and find it easier to develop social skills and self-reliance where they are expected to take more responsibility for their own behaviour. Some people also feel that it's easier to be creative in less formal environments.

Boarding schools www.darch.co.uk

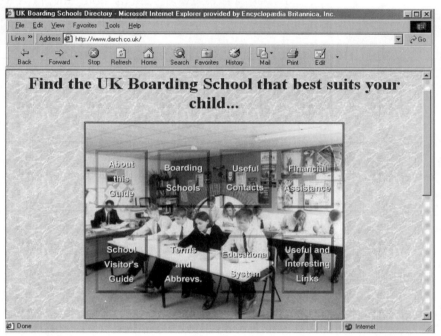

A source of reference for UK boarding schools, this site is intended to help you find the school that best suits your child and also provide related contacts and services. The site is still under development and more schools are being added. To assist your selection of schools there is a data-search facility set up on the first page of the 'Schools Directory'. Each school has a summary sheet giving basic details relating to the school. For some schools more detailed information is available, such as 'Prospectus' and 'Further Information'. There is also an e-mail 'Information Request' facility.

Uniform

Many parents prefer their children to wear school uniform, since they feel it looks smarter, leads to less competition among fashion-conscious kids, and improves morale and pride in the school. Others feel that uniforms aren't really that practical, that they may lead to a loss of individuality, and that children take pride in themselves and their schools for reasons other than the clothes they wear. Some schools have begun to find a middle way, by having a school sweatshirt or tee-shirt, perhaps with a dress code (such as 'no trainers') as well.

WWW
Independent Schools Information Service
www.isis.org.uk

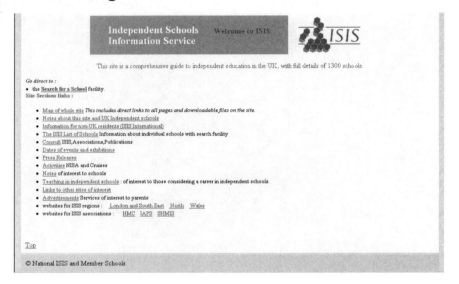

The Independent Schools Information Service site provides a guide to independent education in the UK, with full details of 1300 schools. This site makes available the ISIS database to parents and others looking for information about UK independent schools. Searching facilities are built into the site to allow you to look for schools according to your own requirements. There is also general information about the UK independent sector and advice on how to go about choosing an appropriate school for your child.

WHERE TO FIND OUT ABOUT SCHOOLS

State schools

You should be able to get a list of the schools in your area from your local education authority (LEA), or you could ask at the library, or perhaps the local community centre or health centre. However, you will want much more information before you make a commitment to send your child to a particular school. Sources of information include:

- brochures issued by the schools themselves (ring them and ask for one);
- other local parents and their children (it might be interesting to see how opinions differ!);
- school inspection reports by the Office for Standards in Education (OFSTED) – get them from the schools, from the library or online.

OFSTED **www.ofsted.gov.uk**

The remit of OFSTED is to improve standards of achievement and quality of education through regular independent inspection, public reporting, and informed independent advice. This site describes the organisation of OFSTED, explains how it is managed, and summarises the school inspection system that it operates. A wide variety of information can be downloaded free of charge direct from the site, including past reports for all schools inspected, schedules of future inspections, annual Chief Inspector's reports, and a variety of general reports summarising overall findings in areas such as special needs, able children, ethnic minorities, literacy and numeracy.

Performance tables

Every LEA (Local Education Authority) is required to publish the results of the National Curriculum tests taken at the end of Key Stage 2. These cover mathematics, science and English, and are taken into account when a child moves to secondary school.

There are two kinds of test, and the results of each are published. The first are teacher-assessed, which takes place over a fairly long period of time. The other type are the Standard Attainment Tests (SATs), or national tests, which are sent away to be marked. Children are supposed, on average, to achieve Level 4 by the end of Key Stage 2 (*see* page 38).

It is important to remember that the performance tables only show end results – they don't reflect what stage children were at when they joined a school. For this reason, they can be highly misleading, so although they can be very useful, should be approached with some caution.

The league tables can be accessed online at **www.parents.org.uk**

Independent schools

There are several organisations that can help you get information about independent schools. These are listed below. Before you make a decision – and certainly before you part with any money – you should obtain whatever information for parents the school provides, and arrange to visit. This is especially important if you have decided that your child should go as a boarder.

Key sites for choosing an independent school

- Independent Schools Information Service **www.isis.org.uk** (e-mail: national@isis.org.uk)
- Incorporated Association of Preparatory Schools **www.iaps.org.uk/iapshome.htm** (e-mail: hg@iaps.org.uk)

- Boarding Education Alliance **www.boarding.org.uk/home.htm** (e-mail annwilliamson@classic.msn.com)
- Council of British Independent Schools in the European Communities **www.cobisec.org** (e-mail: cobisec@compuserve.com)
- Girls' Day School Trust **www.gdst.net** (e-mail: reception@wes.gdst.net)

Home schooling

If you've decided to opt for home schooling, or if you are still deciding, you'll probably want information and advice about how to organise things. The organisations listed below can help.

- Home Education Advisory Service **www.heas.org.uk** (e-mail: admin@heas.org.uk)
- *Choice in Education* (magazine for home schoolers) **www.choiceineducation.co.uk**
- Educate OnLine **www.educate.co.uk**
- Education Otherwise (informal networking for home schoolers) **www.education-otherwise.org**
- WES Home School (commercial organisation providing home study courses and tutors) **www.weshome.demon.co.uk/teach.html** (e-mail: office@weshome.demon.co.uk)
- Education Now (organisation promoting flexible education for everyone, including children) **www.education-otherwise.org/ Links/edunow/index1.htm#MEMB**
- Home-education website **www.home-education.org.uk**
- Schoolhouse (home education in Scotland) **www.welcome.to/schoolhouse**

THE SCHOOL VISIT

Once you've looked at the school brochures and consulted the other sources of information, you'll be in a position to make a short list of schools to visit.

Do:

- Make an appointment – and bear in mind that you may not be able to visit the very next day.
- Read the brochure thoroughly beforehand, so you know what to look for and what questions to ask when you visit.
- Talk to other parents in the area to see what they think (you might like to leave this till after your visit, though, so you view the school with an open mind).
- Turn up on time and go to the school secretary's office if there isn't a reception area for parents.

Don't:

- Turn up without an appointment and expect to be shown around.
- Wander around the school unaccompanied.
- Miss your appointment without warning.
- Be antagonistic or timid when asking questions.

Looking around the school

You will probably be shown around the school by the headteacher or deputy headteacher. Trying to find out everything you need to know in one short visit may seem daunting, but you can help yourself to make a good decision if you look for evidence of two basic things: a good atmosphere (though this includes many different things) and a high standard of work.

If you can, try to talk to your child's prospective teacher, as well as other members of staff.

Signs of a happy school with high morale

- A welcoming atmosphere around the school entrance.
- Cheerful, friendly children.
- Staff and children lingering at the end of the day.
- Work that is displayed with pride.

- A relaxed attitude between children and staff and among the staff (not just the teachers, but the secretaries, classroom helpers and other support workers).
- An atmosphere of concentration and hard work (though don't expect absolute silence in most modern primary schools!).
- A high level of parental/carer involvement.

Signs of a school with low morale

- Staff who seem harrassed or unwilling to talk (though most teachers are very busy, so use your judgement).
- Too much noise – particularly shouting (by either the children or the teachers!).
- Poor displays of work, especially if they haven't been changed in a long while.
- Rudeness or hostility on the part of the children.

Signs of high standards of work at the school

- Children who answer and ask questions.
- Children who can explain not only what they are doing, but why.
- Children who aren't afraid to get things wrong once in a while.
- Displays of work and information that have a lot of content.
- Evidence that all the subjects on the National Curriculum are being covered.
- Lots of different kinds of work – such as writing, painting, experiments, and design projects.

Signs of poor standards of work

- Too much work that has obviously just been copied out of books.
- Children who can only give rote answers, which they can't explain.
- Beautiful displays of children's work that actually have very little content.
- A lack of work covering one or more areas of the National Curriculum.
- Children showing an obvious lack of enthusiasm for their work.

Questions to ask your child's prospective teacher

If you can, try to talk to your child's prospective teacher. Some things you might want to find out about are suggested below, but you should also try to decide if this is someone your child (and you!) will like and respect. Quite apart from that, you might want to think about whether there's a good fit in terms of style between your child and the teacher. For instance, some children are shy and will be intimidated by a brusque manner; others are a bit more dominant, and may need a firmer hand or a more formal style.

- **How long has the teacher been in the school? In the teaching profession?** On the plus side, more experienced teachers may know how to handle just about any problem that arises. But they may also have got to the point where they are just teaching the same old thing in the same old way year after year. Newer teachers, on the other hand, may be full of enthusiasm and new ideas; but they may require more support from the school and it may take them a little while to find their feet. If the teacher is in their first year of teaching, the school should be providing them with additional support.
- **How long has this teacher been teaching this year group? Do they want to move to another year group?** It's understandable that teachers need a change now and again, otherwise they may grow stale. The key thing is to make sure your child doesn't end up with a teacher who is desperate for a move.
- **If this isn't a reception class, did the teacher move up with the class last year? Do they expect to do so again next year?** On the plus side, this can make for a stable relationship with a teacher who knows their class really well. On the minus side, when the class does eventually get a new teacher, the break-up can be much more painful than it would otherwise be; and if a particular child doesn't get on with the teacher, both parties can have a very bad time.
- **What does the teacher think of their class? Of their discipline? Of their work?** Try to find out whether the teacher is proud of their class. Compare what the teacher says about the children to what you see going on. Be wary of teachers who can't see problems that are clearly present – but be equally wary of those who are full of negativity, especially if it is not, in your view, justified.

Questions to ask the headteacher

- **Strengths and weaknesses** – asking about the schools strengths is a good place to start, since it will allow the headteacher to talk about areas where they feel relaxed. You can either let this drift into weaknesses (and don't accept the idea that there are none – reading the OFSTED report should have given you a good idea about them) or leave that till later on.
- **Literacy and numeracy** – how is the school implementing the Literacy and Numeracy Hours? Are the teachers enthusiastic about implementing them?
- **Religious education** – how does the school handle religious education? If the school is strongly multicultural, is this reflected in its religious education policy?
- **Physical education** – does the school have a qualified PE teacher? Does it have organised team games? If so, do the teams compete with other schools?
- **Resources** – does the school have a good library? What about computer provision? Science and art? Any other specialties, such as photography?
- **Out of school and after school** – is there an after-school or homework club? Are teachers encouraged to take classes out on day trips; if so, what kind of trips are they – do they have much educational value – and do they use local resources? Are there good links with the local community – arts centres, businesses, and perhaps religious organisations and public services such as the police?
- **Parental involvement** – is there an active Parent–Teacher Association (PTA)? Are parents welcome in the school? What about parent helpers in class?
- **Behaviour and discipline** – does the headteacher consider discipline to be a problem in the school? Does the school have a policy on bullying? Has it ever excluded or expelled a child? In the head's opinion, are there particular kinds of problematic behaviour? Are these on the increase or decrease?
- **Staffing and class sizes** – how are classes organised (some schools mix year groups, for instance)? How big are the classes, and what support (support teachers, special-needs teachers, EAL (English as an additional language) teachers, classroom helpers) do class teachers get? Is here a rapid turnover of staff?

APPLYING FOR A PLACE

In theory, you can apply for a place at any school. In practice, some schools are more popular than others. Your child is more likely to get a place at a popular school if they live close by, and/or if they have a brother or sister already at the school. However, neither of these guarantees a place.

This means it's a good idea to apply for places at more than one school, including the one closest to your home. The individual schools will be able to tell you exactly how to apply.

If you don't get the school of your choice, you can appeal against the decision. If you want to do this, contact your local education authority. A directory of LEA addresses, and websites where available, can be accessed at **www.parents.org.uk**

CHAPTER 3

The National Curriculum

● ● ● ● ● ● ● ● ● ● ● ● ● ● ● ● ● ● ●

The National Curriculum was introduced to ensure that all children in state schools receive the same basic education. It has recently been revised to make it clearer and more flexible, and to emphasise that all children – regardless of background or ability levels – are entitled to a high standard of teaching. There's more of an emphasis than before on teaching skills such as communication across the whole curriculum, and new guidelines in personal, social and health education.

At various stages of their time in school, children are tested to see how well they are doing. You'll be told what level of the National Curriculum your child has achieved. The results not only help teachers see what your child's strengths and weaknesses are, but also help them assess their own performance.

National Curriculum **www.nc.uk.net**

This is the official site for the National Curriculum. You can read and download the actual words. Although clearly aimed at teachers, parents who take an active interest in what their children actually do at school will find a considerable amount of useful information. The site is sensibly arranged by subject. In late 1999 revisions to the National Curriculum to be implemented over several years were announced. The site includes the latest version of the Curriculum. Finally, there are links to the corresponding sites for Northern Ireland, Scotland and Wales.

National Curriculum online

Site map
What has changed
To buy a copy
Download and print

Search ICT themes

Help
The purpose of this site
What's new
Feedback

QCA

About the National Curriculum for England
■ English
■ Mathematics
■ Science
■ Design and technology
■ Information and communication technology
■ History
■ Geography
■ Modern foreign languages
■ Art and design
■ Music
■ Physical education
■ Citizenship
□ PSHE

In response to overwhelming demand, this site now features Acrobat pdf files of all the National Curriculum books. These files give you the user-friendly design style of the print edition, in an edition optimised for photocopying or personal printout. Files suitable for use in your word processor are also still available. Go to the download and print area.

Link to DfEE QCA
other useful links
© HMSO
Designed by C21

Raising Standards

www.open.gov.uk

Northern Ireland   Scotland   Wales

WHAT THE NATIONAL CURRICULUM COVERS

Although your child will move through school year by year, the National Curriculum is arranged in broader segments.

The period from your child's third birthday till the end of the reception class is called the Foundation Stage. The rest of your child's time in school is divided into four Key Stages. Only Key Stages 1 and 2 are taught in primary school.

• Key Stage 1 covers what a child aged from five to seven should know, and is taught in Years 1 and 2.
• Key Stage 2 covers what a child aged from seven to eleven should know, and is taught in Years 3 to 6.

Table 3.1 The four Key Stages of the National Curriculum

Key Stage	KS 1	KS 2	KS 3	KS4
Age	5–7	7–11	11–14	14–16
Year groups	1–2	3–6	7–9	10–11
National Curriculum core subjects				
English	X	X	X	X
Mathematics	X	X	X	O
Science	X	X	X	O
National Curriculum foundation subjects				
Design and technology	X	X	X	O
Information and communication technology	X	X	X	X
History	X	X	X	
Geography	X	X	X	
Modern foreign languages			X	O
Art and design	X	X	X	
Music	X	X	X	
Physical education	X	X	X	O
Citizenship			>	>
Statutory from August 2000		X		
Statutory from August 2001		O		
Statutory from August 2002		>		

What must be taught in schools

The Foundation Stage covers six areas of learning:

- personal, social and emotional development
- language and literacy
- mathematical development
- knowledge and understanding of the world
- physical development
- creative development.

By the end of the Foundation Stage, most children should have reached a stage broadly equivalent to Level 1 of the National Curriculum, though some children will still be working towards it, and some will have exceeded it.

Ten subjects must be taught in primary schools from Year 1 on. They are divided up into core and foundation subjects. You'll find more information about what your child will learn in each subject on pages 38 to 78.

The core subjects are:

• English
• mathematics
• science.

The Foundation Subjects are:

• information and communication technology
• history
• geography
• design and technology
• art
• music
• physical education.

Three subjects don't appear on this list:

• modern languages
• religious education
• personal, social and health education.

Modern languages are not required until secondary school (though guidelines are available for primary schools that want to teach them at Key Stage 2). If you want to help your child learn a language before secondary school, **http://www.linguanet.org.uk** may be a useful starting point.

Religious education and the new subject personal, social and health education are slightly different from the other subjects. religious education is compulsory, but schemes of work are agreed locally; these are expected to reflect the idea that Britain's religious traditions are mainly Christian, while taking into account other major religions. The aim is to help children develop spiritually as well as to teach them about the various world religions.

The guidelines for personal, social and health education are a framework, rather than a legal requirement. They are supposed to help schools develop an ethos in which children grow up into healthy, well-balanced and responsible adults. In particular, children should be encouraged to:

- Develop a sense of self, including their strengths and weaknesses, their will to achieve, and a sense of the importance of their own inner lives.
- Understand the difference between right and wrong; develop empathy for others and the desire to do what is right; reflect on the consequences of their actions, and be willing to take responsibility for them.
- Develop a sense of themselves as a member of a family and a community, with rights and responsibilities; be willing to participate and work for the common good.
- Aquire an understanding of cultural traditions and an ability to appreciate and respond to a variety of aesthetic experiences; acquire a respect for their own culture and that of others, an interest in others' ways of doing things and curiosity about differences; develop the knowledge, skills, understanding, qualities and attitudes they need to understand, appreciate and contribute to culture.

All primary schools have to provide a written statement of their policy on sex education, but this does not mean they have to teach it. As a parent, you are entitled to see the policy, and to withdraw your child from sex education if you wish to do so.

LoveLife www.lovelife.hea.org.uk

If the thought of sex education fills you with fear and you have concerns over approaching the subject with your children, this could be the site for you. With its funky name and style, this is the Health Education Authority site for sex education. Definitely aimed at the older child, it truly confronts this difficult subject head on. There is plenty of practical advice, even how to use a condom. The safer-sex game will get teenagers thinking about some of the issues. With its youth cultural focus, this site could help parents deal with sex education by working through the materials and games together.

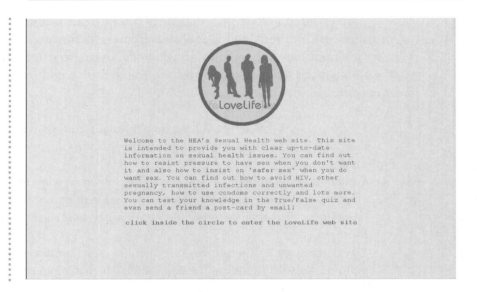

Welcome to the HEA's Sexual Health web site. This site
is intended to provide you with clear up-to-date
information on sexual health issues. You can find out
how to resist pressure to have sex when you don't want
it and also how to insist on 'safer sex' when you do
want sex. You can find out how to avoid HIV, other
sexually transmitted infections and unwanted
pregnancy, how to use condoms correctly and lots more.
You can test your knowledge in the True/False quiz and
even send a friend a post-card by email!

click inside the circle to enter the LoveLife web site

Skills, understanding and knowledge

In each of the ten subjects, children are taught skills, understanding and knowledge.

Skills

These are things children need to be able to do, (for example, how to weigh objects accurately using a set of scales; how to tell the time using a clock; how to look words up in a dictionary).

Check out Parents Online (**www.parents. org.uk**) for a selection of activities for you and your child.

Understanding

This means having a grasp of basic concepts and ideas (for example, writing conveys meaning; water, ice and steam are all forms of the same substance; the difference between living, dead and non-living).

 Discuss and demonstrate the different forms of water: freeze some water to form ice, then boil some water to make steam.

Knowledge

This means knowing things 'off by heart' (for example, historical dates; countries in Europe; how to spell common words). So, your child might have the skill of being able to multiply 8 by 6, know that they equal 48, and understand that multiplication is a process of repeated addition.

 List some common words on a sheet of paper, then once your child has had time to learn these, give them a spelling test.

Learning across the curriculum

Certain key skills are important across the curriculum in providing the basic tools your child will need in order to be able to learn effectively. His teacher will help him develop these skills throughout his work, as well as in specific subject areas such as mathematics and language. They are:

- **Communication** – the ability to speak, write and read effectively.
- **Application of number** – number skills, including mental arithmetic, and the ability to apply them to problem solving; the development of other mathematical skills and concepts.
- **Information technology** – how to choose appropriate sources of information (including websites, CD-ROMs, and other computer-based ones); how to apply the information to problem solving, including recording, analysing, evaluating and presenting it.
- **Working with others** – co-operating with others in a variety of day-to-day and work situations; contributing to problem-solving efforts and discussions; developing an appreciation of different points of view.

- **Improving one's own learning and performance** – learning how to learn – children think about what they have learned, and how they might improve further.
- **Problem solving** – how to identify problems and develop ways of solving them, including monitoring progress and evaluating results.

These key skills are complemented by 'thinking skills', which help children to use the other skills effectively. They include:

- **Information-processing skills** – finding information, and working with it in a variety of ways, such as sorting it or comparing and contrasting.
- **Reasoning skills** – learning how to back up arguments by giving reasons for them, how to make deductions and inferences, and to judge evidence for themselves.
- **Enquiry skills** – identifying problems, asking appropriate questions, planning lines of attack, researching, predicting outcomes and improving results by fair testing.
- **Creative thinking skills** – how to come up with new ideas, to innovate and suggest hypotheses.
- **Evaluation skills** – how to judge the worth of information, opinions, and the work of themselves and others, by developing criteria and applying them.

Finally, schools are expected to provide opportunities for children to learn financial management (how to handle money), enterprise (dealing with change and learning to innovate), and sustainable development (environmental awareness).

Computers can be excellent in developing some of the above skills. For example, devise a family project to produce a report about your house, including measurements (areas and lengths), values and local information. The report could be produced on the computer using a variety of software packages (word processing, spreadsheets, databases etc.) and the internet used for external sources. Finally the report could be formally presented to a group of friends.

Topmarks www.topmarks.co.uk

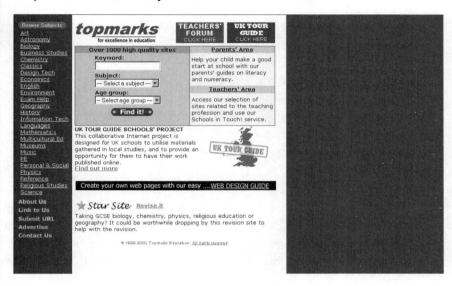

This site describes itself as the UK's favourite educational search engine. It provides links to 1000 educational sites on the web. There are separate areas specifically for teachers and also for parents. Site content focuses on the UK curriculum. The objectives of the site are stated as providing easy access to the best educational web sites, helping teachers use the web in the classroom, providing teachers with web-design guidance and publishing articles for parents to help their children.

ASSESSMENT

Children are assessed when they enter infant school to see what skills, strengths and weaknesses they have. They are given national tests at ages 7 and 11. Parents are told what level their children have achieved in these tests so they can see how well they are doing relative to the national average. You'll find more information about assessment in Chapter 4, or a comprehensive guide at **www.parents.org.uk**

Table 3.2 *Expected levels of attainment*

	Range of levels within which the great majority of pupils are expected to work		Expected attainment for the majority of pupils at the end of the Key Stage
Key Stage 1	1–3	at age 7	2
Key Stage 2	2–5	at age 11	4
Key Stage 3	3–7	at age 14	5/6

ENGLISH

The purpose of teaching English is to help children become literate – that is, to read, write and speak fluently and with confidence. They should learn to express themselves creatively and effectively, and to enjoy a wide variety of books, drama, poetry and non-fiction. They should be able to explain what they thought about what they have experienced, and say why it had that effect on them.

English is important in many areas of the curriculum. It can contribute to your child's personal development and the understanding of many of the key skills. For instance, children can explore moral, spiritual, and social issues through drama and writing, and they can discover more about cultures (their own and others) through reading and watching drama.

The key skill of communication is obviously one where English can help a great deal, since it's all about speaking and listening, reading and writing. English can help with IT by giving children the chance to work on-screen (using word-processing programs, for instance), and use e-mail and the internet. Drama and collaborative writing help children work with each other. The process of doing more than one draft of a piece of work can help them learn to improve their own work. Finally, children can attempt problem solving through group work and drama.

English is also important to thinking skills. For instance, reading widely can help to put issues and problems into context; learning to write and speak effectively involves backing up arguments with solid reasons; discussing books and other pieces of writing involves making value judgements and distinguishing between fact and opinion.

Book Trust **www.booktrust.org.uk**

Book Trust is an independent, educational charity founded to promote books and reading, encouraging readers of all ages and cultures to discover and enjoy books. There is a dedicated area for parents, with plenty of tips to encourage children into books and reading. To get you started there are several suggested books, usefully split across different age ranges.

English is divided into three areas:

- speaking and listening
- reading
- writing.

Speaking and listening

As children progress from infants to top juniors, they will go from talking to each other while they are playing (which, of course, also involves listening), through speaking to the whole class (in activities such as 'News Time'), to holding discussions and debates.

By the time they leave junior school, they should be able to put forward a point of view, listen to other people's arguments and know how to disagree logically and politely. They should understand the difference between an opinion and a fact, and they should know that there are different ways of speaking, and that some of these are more appropriate than others in certain situations.

Encourage your child to give a short daily report on their activities, perhaps at teatime.

Reading

Children will progress from 'pre-reading activities' – learning that writing has meaning, that it goes across the page from left to right, talking about pictures and learning to associate text with them – to being able to sound out words (and recognise some on sight) for themselves. Later, they'll learn to read silently, and to understand more complex texts; they'll learn to read aloud (and in an interesting way!); and they'll learn to use and enjoy a variety of reading materials including fiction, non-fiction, magazines and newspapers. Discussing what they are reading is an important part of all of this. Reading is one of the most important areas parents can help with. It's also one of the easiest and most fun.

A long car journey can present many opportunities for basic reading, for example posters, road and other signs. Make a simple game of spelling a word using the initial letter from road signs.

Writing

There are several aspects to the teaching of writing. One – perhaps the most important, and yet in some ways the easiest to overlook – is that writing is a means to communicate. Although it's important for children to understand grammar and punctuation and to be able to spell and write legibly, these are pretty hollow skills if they don't know how to organise their thoughts or put a point of view across – or if they aren't encouraged to have something to say (whether in fiction or factual writing).

Other aspects of writing are easier to quantify, however. For instance, children start by learning to print, but should be beginning to do 'joined up' writing by the age of seven. As for spelling, though they will probably start by recognising just the first sounds of words, they should progress so that by age seven they are spelling most single-syllable words correctly, and are using common patterns of letters and sounds to help them; by nine, they should be able to spell common words of several syllables correctly.

Children will become familiar with punctuation when they are reading. By seven, they should be using full stops and capital letters; by nine, they should be able to cope with speech marks, exclamation marks and commas.

Encourage regular letter writing, perhaps to a distant relative.

The Literacy Hour

Literacy is considered such an important part of the curriculum that the government has introduced the Literacy Hour to support it. Children spend an hour a day focusing on reading and language skills. The way this time is spent is tightly prescribed:

• For the first 15 minutes children work as a class on a text (fiction or non-fiction). The discussion covers concepts like plot and character, or the way text is laid out and organised.

• In the next 15 minutes the class continues to work together on the same text, but concentrates on words and sentences. For instance, they may talk about verbs and nouns, singular and plural, or adjectives and adverbs.

• For the 20 minutes or so after that, the class breaks up into smaller groups. Some of these will work independently, while the teacher concentrates on leading the others. They will work on activities such as guided reading, creative writing, spelling, and vocabulary extension.

• In the last 10 minutes the class comes back for a 'plenary session', where they discuss the work they did, especially the group work. This is a chance for the teacher to assess how well the children have understood what they have been taught, to clear up any misunderstandings, and to extend some of the concepts that have been introduced.

Many teachers feel that the Literacy Hour has a weak spot, in that it doesn't allow time for extended reading and writing. However, there's nothing to say that time can't be made for these activities in the rest of the school week.

Encourage your child to read regularly at home: join the local library – addresses can be found at online directories such as **www.scoot.co.uk** and **www.yell.co.uk**

Literacy Hour **www.literacyhour.co.uk**

This is a complete resource to support teachers in developing literacy skills within the Literacy Hour at Key Stage 1 and Key Stage 2. Information provided covers shared reading, guided reading, independent reading and language skills. The site provides model lesson plans, organisational ideas and interactive activities for developing language skills through an integrated approach to reading, writing and speaking. The overall objective of the site is to assist teachers in literacy, ensuring pupils read and write with confidence, fluency and understanding, self-monitor their reading and correct their own mistakes, understand the phonics/spelling system and use this to read and spell accurately, develop vocabulary, enjoy reading and writing, develop imagination, inventiveness and critical awareness.

MATHEMATICS

Mathematics gives children a powerful set of tools with which they can understand and change the world. With these, children can solve problems, reason logically and think in abstract ways. Mathematics is important in everyday life, in many forms of employment, and in understanding many aspects of the world, such as economics, the environment and public decision making.

In the primary school, the National Curriculum divides mathematics into three areas:

- number and algebra
- shapes, space and measures
- handling data.

Of these, only the first two are taught at Key Stage 1. The third, handling data, is brought in at Key Stage 2.

Teachers are required to make sure that mathematics is used everywhere it is appropriate across the curriculum. They should also ensure that children learn to apply mathematics to everyday situations, and that they are able to identify and solve problems using the correct mathematical language and skills.

Cooking can be an excellent source of mathematics: get your children to help with measuring and counting ingredients.

Water Counts www.thames-water.com/watercounts

This is a community project sponsored by Thames Water to support the Numeracy Hour. The site contains plenty of water-related facts and figures, with online puzzles and activities to download. Of interest to parents is a section titled 'Home Counts', a guide to help at home with numeracy and how to make numbers fun.

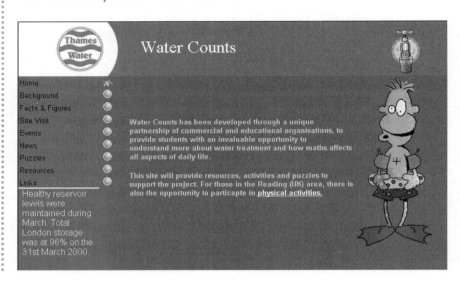

Number and algebra

This area covers counting, adding, subtracting, multiplying and dividing. At Key Stage 2 children learn about decimals and fractions, and simple algebraic ideas. They also learn how data can be represented – and misrepresented. As well as learning tables 'off by heart' (by the end of junior school), they practise mental arithmetic and various ways of writing sums out. They learn how to identify real-world problems and read written ones, and work out how to solve them. They learn how to use mathematical symbols, and how to use language to communicate ideas about number effectively.

Whilst shopping, give the children a set budget, then challenge them to buy a certain number of items. For example, how many tins of beans can they buy for 50p?

Shape, space and measures

This area includes learning about the properties of shapes (such as triangles, squares and rectangles), including their names and what makes them similar to, and different from, each other, and how to recognise relationships between them. It also includes learning about measurement – length, area, volume and weight – how to estimate, and, at Key Stage 2, how to use measuring equipment such as rulers and scales. Finally, it includes learning to tell the time. Children learn to identify and tackle problems involving shapes, measurement and time, and how to use appropriate language to communicate their ideas.

Discuss the shape of various household objects – how many triangles, squares and rectangles can you find in each room.

Handling data

This begins to be taught at Key Stage 2, in the juniors, and includes learning how to collect and sort information, how to present it in graphs and charts, and how to use appropriate mathematical language. Children should learn how to apply these skills in other areas of the curriculum, especially science.

Using a jar to create a simple rainfall meter, record how much rain falls each day over a week. Present the data both as a table and a chart.

Numeracy Hour

The Numeracy Hour is part of the government's National Numeracy Strategy for schools, aimed squarely at raising basic standards. Like the Literacy Hour, it provides a daily framework for teaching.

At Key Stage 1, the 'hour' is more like a 45-minute session, though this does go up to a full hour at Key Stage 2.

- For the first ten minutes, teachers concentrate on oral skills and mental calculations.
- The bulk of the session follows, lasting 30 or 40 minutes. Here, the focus is supposed to be whole class and direct teaching, though there's scope for children to work individually and in pairs or small groups.
- The last 10 minutes rounds up the whole session – children share what they've learned, and any problems are cleared up.

In some schools, this requires a very different approach to classroom organisation. Instead of getting the children to work in small groups, each doing a different task relating to a different aspect of the curriculum, everyone works together on the same basic activity.

Although numeracy is given an hour to itself, teachers are still supposed to relate it to the rest of the curriculum. They have to find ways to integrate mathematical skills into other subject areas. For instance, many Design Technology projects may require children to understand how to measure length and area; or for a science project, children may need to collect data (information) and record it.

For more information on the Numeracy Hour, see **www.educate. org.uk/numeracy.htm**

Maths resources

Useful sites can be found at:

- **www.mathgoodies.com/**
- **www.teachingideas.co.uk/**
- **http://atschool.eduweb.co.uk/ufa10/num_cent.htm**

Maths Net www.anglia.co.uk/education/mathsnet/

This is a site devoted to maths, with plenty of resources, puzzles and games. Of particular interest is the animations section, used to illustrate various mathematical principles.

Maths Year 2000

If you are looking to increase your knowledge, and your family's knowledge of mathematics in the new millennium, Maths Year 2000 will be of interest. The objective is to increase the understanding and awareness of maths for everyone. The project wants to help create a 'let's do – can do' attitude towards maths and give everyone the chance to increase their confidence and maths skills and discover the fun and excitement of numbers.

Maths Year 2000 www.mathsyear2000.org

This site will explain what Maths Year 2000 is all about and help you to get involved. There are loads of events going on all over the country for all ages and abilities, stacked with plenty of inspirational ideas.

Throughout the first year there will be competitions covering maths and art, maths and games, maths and photography, maths and poetry. Get your school signed up with Maths Year 2000 and you will receive lots of free material. Businesses are encouraged to help local schools by joining or forming a mentoring scheme. There are also a growing number of links to other sites supporting the project, many containing excellent numeracy resources.

SCIENCE

Science gives children a set of tools that they can use to understand the world about them in a logical way, using observation, deduction and experimentation. It enables them to understand more about their environment, health and food, and the industrial products they use in everyday life.

Your child will do simple experiments at school as part of learning about science. His teacher will ensure these are done safely, and will make sure your child learns how to behave so he doesn't put himself or others at risk.

Primary school science is divided into four areas:

• scientific enquiry
• life processes and living things

- materials and their properties
- physical processes

Scientific enquiry

In this area, children are basically taught to think and behave like scientists. They learn to look closely at the world around them, and record what they observe and measure. They learn to ask questions about the world and devise ways of finding out the answers. They make predictions about what they think might happen in different situations and learn to devise fair tests (that is, ones where the conditions are properly controlled and only one variable is changed at a time), to discover if they are right, and then record the results (which can include drawing, writing and making charts and graphs).

Science Museum www.nmsi.ac.uk

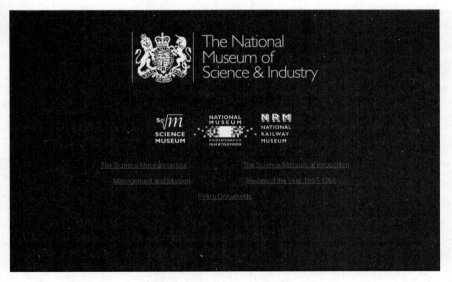

The Science Museum is a family favourite, with plenty of interactive exhibits allowing children to participate in science. As you would expect, this site includes the usual details about the museum, all very useful when planning an actual visit. For most families a visit to the museum will be a rare treat. This site goes a long way to demonstrate how the internet can be used to access some of the treasures throughout the year. Some of the exhibits have been turned into interactive offerings. For example, there is a little game to build an arch bridge, neatly illustrating some of the science behind construction projects.

Life processes and living things

This area is about plants, animals and human beings. Children learn how to group the natural world: about the differences between living things and things that have never been alive; about the differences and similarities between animals and plants; and how different plants and animals are found in different places because of local variations in the environment. They learn about their senses, and that animals need food, water and sleep to survive, and that plants need water and light. At Key Stage 2 – in the Juniors – they go on to learn that people need a good diet and exercise to remain healthy, and they do work on the effects of drugs such as tobacco and alcohol. They learn how animals and plants reproduce – and humans too. The school may wish to discuss with you – perhaps at a special meeting – what they plan to do, so that everyone is happy about it.

WWW

Naturenet www.naturenet.net

naturenet

Countryside Management & Nature Conservation

Ask the Ranger!
The answers to your questions

Conservation Designations
Types of special and protected areas

Countryside Law
Get to know your stuff – it's all here.

Rights of Way
Get out and about: it's your right!

Agencies and Organisations
involved with the countryside

Environmental Education
Teaching in the natural environment

Careers and Training
Do you fancy working in conservation?

Volunteer!
Time to get your wellies on!

Biodiversity
The variety of life – and the legislation that goes with it

Opinion
Our writers sound off

A UK site for those interested in nature and their environment. Plenty of links, including online nature reserves. The directory of appropriate organisations may be useful if you want to get involved with conservation.

Materials and their properties

This area teaches children about everyday materials such as wood, metal, plastics and paper. Your child will learn to sort materials according to their properties (such as weight, flexibility, stretchiness and so on), and learn the proper vocabulary to describe them. She will learn that some materials change when they are heated or mixed with water, and that some of these changes are reversible and some are irreversible, and that there are differences between solids, liquids and gases. She will learn that some materials are better for certain jobs than others (such as thermal insulation or as electrical conductors), and how to explain this or justify her choices.

Find a selection of different materials from around the house, such as bricks, wood, paper, plastic. Discuss their various properties, then sort by these.

Physical processes

In this area children learn about the processes and forces that affect materials. These include light, sound, electricity and forces such as friction, acceleration and vibration. Your child will investigate the properties of sound, such as pitch and volume; learn to make simple (and, eventually, more complex) electrical circuits (with appropriate warnings about the dangers of playing with mains electricity!); and set up experiments to discover what makes objects move, stop, speed up and change direction. He will investigate light and shadow, and learn how the movement of the Sun, Earth and Moon affects us.

Explore Science www.explorescience.com

This large US site takes various scientific concepts and creates multi-media experiments that can be experienced online. For example, you can simulate what happens when two balls collide, changing their relative directions and angles to discover how these factors affect the post-collision direction. There are also fun games, again illustrating different scientific principles.

Bath time can be a great opportunity for *ad hoc* science experiments. For example, the rise and fall of the water level as the children get in and out of the bath can be used to demonstrate displacement.

INFORMATION AND COMMUNICATION TECHNOLOGY

Information and communication technology (ICT) enables children to use computers, software and other electronic devices (such as video recorders) to help them find information, and explore, analyse, evaluate, and exchange it, as well as using it to solve problems. ICT also helps to broaden children's experience of the world by giving them access to ideas and experiences from different people and communities. Becoming familiar with this kind of equipment allows children to judge when it can be used to best effect.

ICT is not intended to replace reading, writing and basic maths skills such as arithmetic, but to complement it – providing a sound basis that children can build on in secondary school, so that they understand how computers and information technology are used in industry and the workplace.

ICT is divided into four areas:

- finding things out
- developing ideas and making things happen
- exchanging and sharing information
- reviewing, modifying and evaluating work as it progresses.

Finding things out

Children learn how to gather information from a variety of sources, such as people, books, CD-ROMs, video and TV. They learn how to store it in a variety of ways, including on computer disks, and how to retrieve it afterwards. At Key Stage 2 they learn how to define the information they need more closely, how to check it for accuracy and classify it, and how to interpret it and decide if it is relevant to the task at hand.

Use the internet to research your next holiday destination: can you find out how many people live in the area and any famous attractions?

Parents Information Network **www.pin.org.uk**

PIN is an independent organisation established in 1994 to provide information and advice to parents about the role of computers in their children's education. The site contains a wealth of advice on using computers, with a vast database of reviews of many of the leading educational software titles.

Parents
Information
Network

PIN is an independent organisation established in 1994 to provide information and advice to parents about the role of computers in their children's education. PIN believes it is vital for parents to have an understanding of how they can support their children in this new and powerful area of learning. To this end, PIN also works with teachers who wish to extend support to parents in the rapidly growing area of computers and education.

Parents

Teachers

Developing ideas and making things happen

Children learn how to develop their ideas using text, tables and images, selecting from the information they have gathered and adding to it as necessary, and trying things out to see what will happen in real and imaginary situations (for example, using simulations or adventure games). They learn how to plan and give instructions in order to make things happen (for example, by using programmable electronic toys). They learn to monitor and evaluate the responses they get, and to explore computer models and simulations, and to investigate patterns and relationships.

See **www.parents.org.uk** for product reviews.

Exchanging and sharing information

Children learn to share information in a variety of ways – for example, by using text, images, tables, and sounds (and, at Key Stage 2, e-mail and multimedia) – and to present their finished work effectively. They learn to take the needs of specific audiences into account (for example, the difference between preparing work to help children younger than they are, for a school assembly, or for publication on the internet).

 Find out which of your relatives have an e-mail address and encourage the children to e-mail them regularly.

Reviewing, modifying and evaluating work as it progresses

Children learn to review what they and others have done in order to develop their ideas, to discuss the impact it has on others, and to consider other media they might have used. They learn to talk about what they might do differently in future, and what improvements they could make.

HISTORY

Children are taught history so that they can develop an understanding of the past and the way it affects the present, of cause and effect, and of how the world they live in came about. They build up a chronological framework into which they can fit their knowledge of significant events and people. Through learning about earlier societies and people, children develop an understanding of different beliefs and ways of living. Not only is this interesting in its own right, it can also help children develop emotionally, morally, and spiritually.

The study of history involves the skills of gathering, analysing and evaluating information, as well as reaching conclusions, presenting them to other people, and backing them up with reasoned arguments.

In the primary school, the study of history is divided into various types of skill:

• chronological understanding
• knowledge and understanding of events, people and changes in the past
• historical interpretation
• historical enquiry
• organisation and communication.

These skills are developed through the study of the different periods and societies laid down by the National Curriculum.

SCRAN www.scran.ac.uk

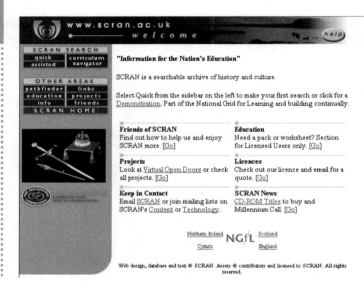

SCRAN is a massive searchable database of history and culture. Although much of the content is of a Scottish origin, it is still of interest to others. The site allows you to search in a number of different ways, for example, using a specific date range. This is particularly useful if you are doing a project on a particular year. For schools, a licence can be purchased gaining access to a wide variety of educational resources.

Chronological understanding

Children learn to place events and objects in chronological order, and to use the correct language to describe the passing of time. At Key Stage 2 they will also learn to place events, people and changes into the correct periods, and to use dates and more advanced language to describe the passing of time.

Create a family tree on a large sheet of paper, then using the internet and other reference sources, research key events for each birth date.

Knowledge and understanding of events, people and changes in the past

Children learn to identify different ways of life; later they learn about the characteristic features of different periods and societies, including the beliefs, attitudes, and ways of life of the people who lived in them. They learn to recognise why people did things, why events happened, and what the outcomes of these were. They learn to describe and make links between the main events and situations in the periods and societies studied.

Historical interpretation

Children learn to recognise the different ways in which the past is represented, and (at Key Stage 2) to give reasons for different interpretations of history.

Historical enquiry

Children learn to gather information from a range of sources. These might include books and other printed sources, music, photographs, CD-ROMs, visits to museums, galleries and sites, and looking at artefacts. They learn to ask and answer questions, and to communicate information.

English Heritage **www.english-heritage.org.uk** has a comprehensive listing of historical attractions to visit. Devise a project out of a visit to one of these; if time allows, this could include pre-visit investigations using the web and a post-visit report.

Organisation and communication

Children learn to select information from what they know, and communicate it in different ways using appropriate language. They learn about a selection of societies and periods. Your child's school has some leeway in its selection, but it must include:

At Key Stage 1

- Changes in your child's own life, your family, and the people around you.
- The way of life of people in the past in Britain, either locally or elsewhere.
- The lives of significant people in the history of Britain and elsewhere – for instance, artists, explorers, inventors, pioneers.
- Historical events from Britain and the world – for instance, the Gunpowder Plot, the Olympic Games.

At Key Stage 2

- A local history study, showing either how the area has developed over a long period, or how it was affected by a single national or local event, or a significant event.
- British history – including the study of the Romans, Anglo-Saxons and Vikings; Britain and the world in Tudor times; and either Victorian Britain or Britain since 1930.
- The people of Ancient Greece, and their way of life, and how their beliefs and achievements still influence the world today.
- World history – a study of the ways of life of the people of either Ancient Egypt, Ancient Sumer, the Assyrian Empire, the Indus Valley, the Maya, the Benin or the Aztecs.

DESIGN AND TECHNOLOGY

Design and technology teaches children how to design and make things. In order to do this, they must find ways to solve problems creatively, looking at the needs of individuals and groups, and they must evaluate their results, taking into account aesthetics, social and environmental issues, and functionality. These skills are important because they provide a basis on which children can build in secondary school, allowing them to understand the engineering, manufacturing and other processes that are vital in industry and the workplace.

Design and technology is divided up into various components:

- developing, planning and communicating ideas
- working with tools, equipment, materials and components to make quality products
- evaluating processes and products
- knowledge and understanding of materials and components.

How Stuff Works www.howstuffworks.com

This is a great site for finding out how things work. Everyday objects are explained in some detail, often with suitable illustrations. This site would be very useful when discussing objects around the home. Also covered are sections on the weather, time and even how Christmas 'works'.

Developing, planning and communicating ideas

Children study products in order to understand them (for example, by taking them apart). They draw on their own and other people's experiences; develop ideas by shaping materials and putting together components; design their own products with an eye to their usefulness and aesthetic value; communicate their plans and ideas; evaluate how successful they have been; and work out how to improve on their work.

Working with tools, equipment, materials and components to make quality products

Children explore the use of a wide variety of materials (such as flexible and stiff sheet materials, including wood, plastic and fabric; materials that can be moulded, such as dough and clay; construction kits; electrical components; and materials that can be used to make frameworks). They select appropriate tools and techniques for making their products, and explore alternative methods they could use. They learn how to assemble components and finish their products well.

Get the children to help you with all those DIY jobs around the house, don't forget safety.

Evaluating processes and products

Children learn to discuss their plans and what they could have done differently. They learn to test their work and to recognise that its quality depends on how well it meets its intended purpose.

Examine and discuss everyday objects – could you improve on the design?

Knowledge and understanding of materials and components

Children explore the characteristics of different materials and how they can be used and adapted. They investigate ways of making things move and how to control them (using, for example, computer programs or electrical switches).

Children develop all these areas through investigating and evaluating everyday products, discovering how well they work and what people think about them. They design and make products of their own, using a range of materials (such as food, mouldable materials, sheet materials, textiles and electrical and mechanical components).

Using old boxes, packaging and cotton reels build a model car. A cereal box can be used as the body, cotton reels with sticks for wheels.

GEOGRAPHY

Children study geography to help them understand the world in which they live – both their local environment and the wider world. Geography provides a focus for understanding issues surrounding the environment and sustainable development, and for developing a knowledge of places throughout the world using a variety of investigative and problem-solving approaches. It is an important link between the social and natural sciences and as such provides inspiration for children to consider their own place in the world, their values, the way in which they want to live, and their rights and responsibilities in relation to other people and the environment.

The teaching of geography in primary schools is broken down into several components, including skills and areas of knowledge and understanding. These are developed through the study of different geographical areas and themes. They include:

- geographical enquiry and skills
- knowledge and understanding of places
- knowledge and understanding of patterns and processes
- knowledge and understanding of environmental change and sustainable development.

Atlapedia www.atlapedia.com

An online atlas from around the world containing both physical and political maps. There are also facts, figures and statistical data on geography, climate, people, religion, language, history, and economy for each individual country.

Atlapedia Online contains full color physical and political maps as well as key facts and statistics on countries of the world.

The **Countries A to Z** section, provides facts, figures and statistical data on geography, climate, people, religion, language, history, economy & more..for each individual country.

The **World Maps** section, provides full color physical and political maps for regions of the world.

Don't forget to Bookmark this page now. Why not tell your teachers and friends about this site too.

Geographical enquiry and skills

Children learn to ask geographical questions (for example, 'What is it like to live here?'). They observe and record geographical evidence and analyse it – for example, by comparing and contrasting information from two different areas – and draw conclusions from it. They form opinions about people, places and environments, and topical geographical issues, and express them in various ways. They identify and explain other people's points of view on these issues and they learn to make decisions bearing in mind what they have discovered.

They communicate their findings and opinions in a variety of ways, taking into account their audience. In doing all this, they learn to use appropriate geographical language, fieldwork techniques and equipment (such as maps, globes, rain gauges, cameras). Where necessary, they make use of secondary sources of information (such as the internet, books, photographs and satellite images). They learn to use and draw maps and plans at different scales.

Using the internet, research life in another country, make comparisons with your own experiences.

Knowledge and understanding of places

Children learn to identify where places are (for example, using maps or descriptions) and what they are like. They recognise how places have become the way they are and how they are changing, and compare them to other places. They recognise how places are linked to other places in the world (for example, by the import of food).

In the kitchen look at the labels of food and other products to find their countries of origin. Create a list of products and their countries, then using an atlas mark where they all come from. Which product has travelled the furthest distance?

Knowledge and understanding of patterns and processes

Children make observations about where things are located and why, about seasonal changes, and about other features of the environment. They learn to recognise changes in the natural and built environment. At Key Stage 2 they learn to recognise some physical and human processes, and explain how these can cause changes in places and environments.

Knowledge and understanding of environmental change and sustainable development

Children learn how people can improve or damage their environment, and how decisions about places and environments can affect the future quality of people's lives. They learn how and why people choose to manage environments sustainably, and identify opportunities for their own involvement.

Regional and thematic studies

At Key Stage 1 children study two localities – the area around their school and a place either in the UK or abroad with physical or human features that contrast with those near the school. Children study at the local scale, and do investigations outside the classroom.

At Key Stage 2, children study a locality in the UK and one abroad that is less economically developed. They also study water and its effects on landscapes and people, how settlements differ and change over time, and an issue caused by a change in an environment, together with attempts to manage the environment in a sustainable way. Children study at a range of scales – local, regional and national; they study a range of places and environments in different parts of the world; and they carry out investigations outside the classroom.

Draw a local map.

ART

Art in primary schools includes art, craft and design. It stimulates creativity and the imagination, and provides a unique way for children to respond to the world around them and communicate their feelings to others. It is taught so that children learn how to express their feelings and thoughts in a variety of ways, using appropriate skills, methods and materials. They also explore the work of other artists, so that they can develop an appreciation of it – that is, not only to enjoy it, but to understand what the artists were hoping to achieve and how they went about it, and how the work enriches our lives.

The curriculum covers:

- exploring and developing ideas
- investigating and making art, craft, and design
- evaluating and developing work
- knowledge and understanding

Exploring and developing ideas

Children learn to observe the world around them, and to record from first-hand observation and their imagination. They collect visual and other information, and select ideas to use in their work.

Drawings and paintings of your house and family can be fun for all ages.

Investigating and making art, craft and design

Children explore the use of different kinds of material, including paper, clay, paint, crayons and fabric in order to express their feelings and thoughts, and to make representations of what they see around them, choosing appropriate materials and methods and using them safely. They learn to work from observation and their imagination, and to interpret their ideas using processes like painting, modelling, printing and collage. They learn to produce surface effects like shade and pattern and explore their effects; and they learn about colour and how to mix it. Finally, they learn how to plan their work, to modify their plans as the work progresses, and to evaluate the finished produt.

Use papier mâché (newspaper, flour and water for the glue) to create models; complexity can be tailored to the age and ability of the child. On completion, these can be painted and/or coloured with felt-tip pens.

www Origami www.geocities.com/Athens/Academy/4800

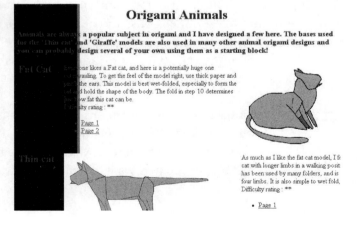

Origami Animals

Animals are always a popular subject in origami and I have designed a few here. The bases used for the 'Thin cat' and 'Giraffe' models are also used in many other animal origami designs and you can probably design several of your own using them as a starting block!

Fat Cat

Everyone likes a Fat cat, and here is a potentially huge one ... crawling. To get the feel of the model right, use thick paper and ... the ears. This model is best wet-folded, especially to form the ... hold the shape of the body. The fold in step 10 determines just how fat this cat can be.

Difficulty rating : **

Page 1
Page 2

As much as I like the fat cat model, I fi cat with longer limbs in a walking posit has been used by many folders, and is four limbs. It is also simple to wet fold, Difficulty rating : **

• Page 1

Thin cat

This is a site dedicated to the art of paper folding. Not only are there a wealth of photographs of fantastic origami models but also introductory tips on doing your own paper folding.

Evaluating and developing work

Children learn to compare ideas and methods in their own and other's work, and say what they think about them. They should learn to adapt their work and describe how they could develop it further.

Knowledge and understanding

Children learn about visual and tactile elements, including colour, pattern and texture, line and tone, shape, form and space. They explore the materials and processes used in making craft, art and design. They study the work of artists and craftspeople from a range of times, cultures and artistic traditions and schools. They discuss their similarities and differences, and begin to learn to distinguish the work of one time period from that of another; they consider what the artist might have been trying to do and how well they have achieved their goals. They learn to express (verbally, in writing, and by producing their own art) the impression (thoughts and feelings) the art has had on them.

Children develop in all these areas by making a range of art, craft and design projects, using a variety of starting points, materials, methods and approaches. They work alone and in collaboration, in both two-dimensions and three-dimensions, and at a range of scales. They investigate the work of others by looking at original and reproduction artwork in a variety of genres, styles and traditions, by visiting museums and galleries, and by looking at sites on the internet.

Virtual Library **www.icom.org/vlmp** contains a comprehensive directory of online museums, art galleries and museum-related resources. Many of these have virtual exhibits, or you may want to arrange an actual visit.

MUSIC

Children learn music in school because it is a unique form of communication – one that brings together intellect and feeling, and contributes to personal expression and emotional development. Children learn to express themselves by singing or playing instruments; and develop an appreciation of music composed and performed by others.

Children must learn the following:

- controlling sound through singing and playing
- creating and developing musical ideas
- responding and reviewing
- listening and applying knowledge and understanding.

Controlling sound through singing and playing – performing skills

Children are given the opportunity to make music by singing and playing instruments (at first unpitched, such as tambourines and drums; later, they will use pitched instruments, such as recorders). They will explore rhythm, tempo and duration; the qualities of sound, such as timbre, dynamics (loud, quiet, silence) and pitch; and the structure of pieces of music (for instance, how to give a piece a beginning, middle and end). They will explore ways of combining these to make different effects singly and in large and small groups. Later, they will learn the skills of musical notation, moving toward being able to read music, and will learn more about melody and accompaniment. They will learn to discuss their work using appropriate vocabulary, improve their work, rehearse it and perform for an audience (such as parents at the end-of-term play, perhaps!).

Listen to different types of music at home.

Creating and developing musical ideas – composing skills

Children learn how to create musical patterns, and how to explore, choose, and organise sounds and musical ideas. They learn to improvise and develop rhythmic and melodic material whilst performing. They explore musical structures, choosing and combining musical ideas.

 Make simple musical instruments from houshold items: for example drums from tins, pipes from bottles. Then see if you can play a well-known tune such as Jingle Bells.

Responding and reviewing – appraising skills

Children listen to music from all over the world, and of all types – classical, folk and popular. They explore the way it makes them feel – perhaps by dancing or painting, as well as by writing, talking and making more music – and later, consider how well the composers achieved the effects they wanted. They learn to recognise different musical instruments, and to discuss why they were used, and explore how different kinds of music reflect different places, cultures and times.

Listening and applying knowledge and understanding

Children learn to listen with attention to detail, and to remember what they hear. They explore how the different musical elements, such as pitch, duration and tempo, can be combined within musical structures to obtain different effects. They learn about the different ways music is created, and how it can vary depending on time and place. They learn how music can be recorded, using their own and standard musical notations.

Children's understanding of music in the primary school is developed through a range of activities that involve and combine performing, composing and appraising. Children listen and respond to many different kinds of music, and use a range of musical and non-musical starting points for their own work. They work alone and in groups of different sizes.

Early Birds Music www.earlybirdsmusic.com/

This is a site of children's music with lots of fun songs and cartoons. Many of these have been illustrated with animated actions and include Real Audio files to allow you to download the actual songs.

MP3 music

If you like music, then you'll find vast resources on the internet. MP3 is a digital audio format that allows pieces of music to be compressed into very small files so they can be moved around easily on the internet by downloading or e-mailing, without having to wait for ages for files to transfer. You can play MP3 files on your computer, or download them into portable personal-stereo sized devices to take with you on your travels. Music can be bought and downloaded from the web, but there's also a lot of music that can be downloaded free of charge. Remember, although it's legal to create your own MP3s and keep them to yourself, it is illegal to trade copyrighted songs with others unless you have special permission from the copyright holder of the song. To learn more about MP3 and how to find music on the web, go to any of the major internet search engines and type in MP3, or try some of the following sites:

- **www.mp3.com** – mp3.com has thousands of songs available for free download. This site features hundreds of artists and labels.
- **www.mp3now.com/html/mp3_search.html** – The top 30 MP3 search engines
- **www.mp3yes.com** – MP3 news, downloads, freebies, beginners' guide etc.

Multimedia **www.tunes.com**

An aggregation of multimedia assets and artist information, featuring original daily editorial content, databases of artist discographies, biographies, interviews, tour dates and music videos, as well as a downloadable photo library of bands, artists and concerts. Its 'Virtual Venue' allows users to see and hear streaming audio (so you can hear sound files before they have completely downloaded) and video web-casts of live and archived concerts.

PHYSICAL EDUCATION

Children are taught physical education (PE) in primary school so that they develop physical competence and confidence, good movement skills, and so that they learn to co-operate and compete with good grace. PE provides opportunities for pupils to be creative and to tackle challenges individually and in groups. Finally, it promotes a positive attitude towards healthy and active lifestyles.

There are various components in the teaching of PE, which are developed across a range of physical activities:

- acquiring and developing skills
- selecting and applying skills, tactics and compositional ideas
- evaluating and improving performance
- knowledge and understanding of fitness and health.

Acquiring and developing skills

Children explore basic skills, actions and ideas with increasing control and co-ordination.

Ball games can be easily played in the garden or park and introduce many different skills.

Selecting and applying skills, tactics and compositional ideas

Children explore how to choose and apply skills and actions in sequence and combination, and to vary the way they perform skills by using simple tactics and movement phrases. They learn to plan and use strategies, tactics and compositional ideas for individual and group activities in order to improve their effectiveness. They apply the rules and conventions for different activities.

Teaching Ideas **www.teachingideas.co.uk/**

A site for primary school teachers with lots of lesson ideas, including a range of PE activities. This site could be of use at home as well.

Evaluating and improving performance

Children learn to describe what they have done, to observe, describe and copy what others have done, and to use what they have learned to improve the quality and control of their work. They learn to identify what makes a performance effective, and to suggest improvements based on this information.

Encourage your child to support and follow a local sports team. See Chapter 8 for more suggestions.

Knowledge and understanding of fitness and health

Children learn about the short-term effects of exercise and why physical activity is good for their health and well-being. They learn to warm up and prepare for different activities, and why wearing appropriate clothing and being hygienic is good for them.

What to expect your child to do in PE

In the infants (Key Stage 1), children learn games, gymnastics and dance; in the juniors (Key Stage 2), they continue with these and athletics, plus outdoor/adventure activities and swimming are added. Some schools may choose to teach swimming at Key Stage 1.

Games

Children develop the skills of physical agility (such as running and dodging) and ball skills, such as throwing and catching, working singly and in small and larger groups. They explore different kinds of games – in the juniors these will include simplified and/or cut-down versions of familiar team sports such as netball, football, rounders and cricket – and develop their knowledge of the tactics needed to play them, such as attacking and defending. They will learn to work with others to keep the games going.

Gymnastics

Children learn to move in a controlled way on the floor and on various pieces of gymnastic equipment. They explore travelling and balancing in various ways using their hands and feet. They learn how to develop sequences of movements that incorporate variations of speed, direction and level, and how to rehearse and perform them.

Dance

Children explore ways of responding to music imaginatively, by moving in controlled ways such as skipping, turning, jumping and balancing. They learn to change the rhythm, speed and direction of their movements in order to express their feelings and reflect the mood of the music. They will also learn some traditional dances, and use movement patterns from different times, places and cultures.

Athletics

Children develop the skills of running, jumping and throwing. They take part in and design challenges that call for precision, speed and power or stamina. They are encouraged to try to improve their personal performances and to pace themselves.

Outdoor and adventurous activities

Children explore outdoor activities. For example, they may be taught orienteering – how to find their way around an area (the school playground, a local park or other suitable place) by using maps, compasses and following directions. They may learn to negotiate obstacle courses both individually and in small groups. In all cases children are encouraged to develop initiative, problem-solving skills and group co-operation.

Swimming

Children are helped to become confident in the water and to understand and practise water safety. They learn how to float, tread water and swim using a variety of strokes and recognised arm and leg patterns. By the end of Key Stage 2, children should be able to swim at least 25 metres unaided.

PERSONAL, SOCIAL AND HEALTH EDUCATION

Personal, social and health education (PSHE) is not a statutory requirement in the National Curriculum, but all schools are expected to develop an ethos based around the framework explained below.

PSHE helps children to develop the skills, knowledge and understanding they need to become informed, active, responsible citizens. Children are encouraged to participate fully in the life of their school and community, learning to recognise their own worth, developing ways of working well with others, and taking responsibility for their own actions and learning. They reflect on their experiences, understand how they are developing personally and socially, and think about the spiritual, moral, cultural, and social issues that affect them as they are growing up. They learn about the main political and social institutions, and how they are affected by them, and about the rights and responsibilities that come with being a member of a society.

Children should become aware of:

• developing confidence and responsibility and making the most of their abilities
• preparing to play an active role as citizens
• developing a healthy, safer lifestyle
• developing good relationships and respecting the differences between people.

Developing confidence and responsibility and making the most of their abilities

Children learn to recognise what they like and dislike, what is fair and unfair, and what is right and wrong. They share their opinions through talking and writing, and explain why they hold them. They set simple goals for themselves, learn from their experiences, recognise what they are good at, and learn to deal with their feelings in a positive way. They also recognise when they have made mistakes, and make amends for them. They face new challenges positively, by collecting information, looking for help and taking action.

As they approach puberty, they learn how it changes people's emotions, and how to deal with this. They learn about the range of jobs people do, and to understand how they can develop skills that will help them in the future. They learn to look after their money, and the value of saving.

Preparing to play an active role as citizens

Children learn to take part in discussions and debates about increasingly complex topical issues. They explore why rules are necessary, why and how rules and laws are made, and what happens when they are broken. They learn about the consequences of negative behaviour such as bullying, aggression and racism, on individuals and societies. They use their imaginations to try to understand other people's experiences, and to appreciate the range of national, regional, religious and ethnic identities in the UK. They learn that they are part of various groups and communities, how they can contribute to them, and how people look after the natural and built environment. They learn about social institutions such as pressure groups and voluntary organisations, and explore the different ways resources can be allocated. They look at the ways the media presents information.

Institute for Citizenship www.citizen.org.uk

The aim of the Institute for Citizenship is to promote informed active citizenship and greater participation in democracy and society. The site contains details and background to the organisation's educational programmes for all ages.

Institute for Citizenship

Home
Citizenship Education
Voter Participation
Stimulating Debate
Press
Links

INSTITUTE FOR
CITIZENSHIP

The aim of the Institute for Citizenship is to promote informed active citizenship and greater participation in democracy and society.

Active citizenship can be as straightforward as helping a neighbour. It can be as challenging as orchestrating a major campaign. For some it comes naturally, perhaps as a result of family tradition, a chance meeting, or an inspirational teacher. For many it needs to be encouraged, practised, developed and informed.

We can't *be* active citizens without *doing* something. We also can't become active without some practical experience. That's why the citizenship education projects that the Institute develops concentrate upon practical ways in which young people can participate as active citizens.

Developing a healthy, safer lifestyle

Children learn about their bodies and the changes that affect them as they grow up and grow old. They learn how to maintain personal hygiene, and how some diseases spread and can be controlled. They learn that all household products, including medicines, can be harmful if not used properly. At Key Stage 2 children learn how to make choices regarding the benefits of exercise and healthy eating, and what affects mental health. They learn about the onset of puberty, about hygiene, and which commonly available substances are legal and illegal and what the effects and risks of using them are. They learn to assess the risks involved in different situations, and how to behave responsibly. They explore ways of recognising peer pressure and how to resist pressure to do wrong. They learn school rules about health and safety, basic emergency-aid procedures, and where to get help.

 Keep an exercise chart, recording times and distances.

Developing good relationships and respecting the differences between people

Children learn to recognise how their behaviour affects other people, how to work and play co-operatively, and that family and friends should care for each other. They also learn the consequences of racism, teasing, bullying and aggressive behaviours, and how to respond to them and find help. They learn to think about the lives of people in other places and times, with different values and customs; that differences and similarities between people arise from cultural, racial, ethnic, religious, and gender diversity, and also disability, and to challenge stereotypes. They develop an awareness of different types of relationship, including marriage and friendship. They develop the skills to be effective in relationships.

 Depending on the age of the children, discuss issues that may be covered in the news – you may be surprised by the views and opinions that even quite young children may hold.

RELIGIOUS EDUCATION

Religious education must be taught in all schools, even though there are no requirements set down for it in the National Curriculum. This is to allow each LEA to vary what is taught to reflect the needs of the people in its area. You can find out what your LEA expects its schools to teach by asking to see its 'Agreed Syllabus'.

You are likely to find that although there is an emphasis on teaching about Christianity, children are also taught about the other faiths that are present in the UK, such as Judaism, Sikhism, Hinduism, Islam and Buddhism. They will learn about important Christian festivals, and compare them to those of other faiths; and about the Bible and the holy books of the other religions.

Children are encouraged to respect the beliefs of others and to understand the values shared by all the major religions – honesty, caring, forgiveness and justice.

If you do not want your child to take part in religious education, you may request that she be withdrawn from the classes.

Stories to Grow by **www.storiestogrowby.com**

This is a site of moral stories from around the world. The stories come from a wide range of cultures and religions – very useful to illustrate differences from around the world. There are also paper-based games to print out and play.

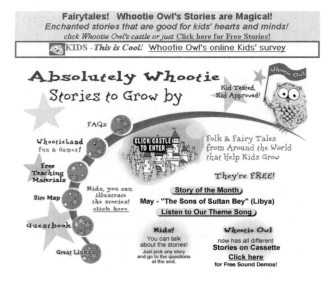

CHAPTER 4

Inspections

● ● ● ● ● ● ● ● ●

OFSTED

The Office for Standards in Education (OFSTED) is responsible for inspecting schools. Each school is seen at least once every six years, though some schools may be seen more often – for example, those that seem to be having difficulties, or that are in a time of transition (when a new headteacher comes in, for example). The inspectors look at the standard of education provided by the school, but also at how well it manages its finances, and what the ethos of the school is like.

The inspectors are independent, though they are trained and accredited by OFSTED. At least one member of each inspection team is a lay person with no experience of teaching or schools' management.

When the inspection is over, the Registered Inspector – the team leader – will write a report about the visit. This, together with a summary, will be sent to the school and also to OFSTED and the LEA. The headteacher must send the full report to the local libraries and media, and a copy of the summary to the parents of every pupil. Parents must be able to get a copy of the full report from the school.

Within 40 working days of the inspection, the school must complete its Action Plan in response to the inspectors' report. This must also be made freely available to parents.

If the inspectors decide that the school is 'failing' – that is, 'failing to give its pupils an acceptable standard of education' – they will say that it is in need of Special Measures. These are designed to bring the school up to scratch by providing it with an Action Plan (approved by the Secretary of State for Education and Employment). This will be closely monitored by inspectors from OFSTED, with reports going to the Secretary of State. This should bring the school back up to standard within two years.

From September 1997 the inspectors have been required to state in their report if they think a school has serious weaknesses, even if it is otherwise providing an acceptable standard of education.

In addition to these general visits, from March to May 2000, every primary school was visited by LEA inspectors, with the aim of helping them set targets to improve performance.

STANDARDISED TESTING

Your child will be given Standard Assessments Tests (SATs) four times while he is in primary school:

- on entering the reception class ('baseline testing')
- at the end of Key Stage 1 (at the end of Infants: the end of Year 2)
- in Year 4
- at the end of Key Stage 2 (at the end of Year 6, before going to secondary school).

The tests help the teachers understand how your child is doing in school, so that they can decide what she needs to learn next. They also help the teachers understand how effective they are being, and what their own strengths and weaknesses are.

The tests are done in May, so it is important to make sure your child is in school then. Parents Online (**www.parents.org.uk**) runs a SATs special in the period leading up to the actual tests, usually at the end of the Spring Term prior to Easter. This includes all the latest SATs news with plenty of practical advice on helping your child through an important period in their education.

THE TESTS

Baseline testing

Unlike the other tests, schools may choose a set of tests from a range approved by the Department for Education and Employment; they will probably use the one recommended by the LEA.

The tests are in:

English (speaking and listening, reading and writing) to see if the child can:

- speak clearly, listen, and hold a conversation;
- read, or have pre-reading skills such as holding a book properly, following a story through pictures, or recognising print;
- write, or have pre-writing skills such as using a pencil, forming letters, etc.

Mathematics (number, shape and space, and measurement) to see if the child can:

- count, recognise numbers and add up;
- recognise shapes and can name them;
- compare the weight and length of objects;
- sort objects by size, colour or shape;
- use some basic mathematical vocabulary.

Personal and Social Development to see if the child can:

- play and work with other children;
- make friends,
- take turns;
- listen to instructions, answer questions and take part in conversations.
- sit quietly and concentrate on a task or story.

End of Key Stage tests

There are two parts to tests at the end of Key Stages:

- **Teacher assessment** – the children are given special tasks to do (individually or in groups) with which the teacher is not allowed to help, and which he marks using a special scheme.
- **National tests** – those children who have done well enough in the teacher assessment go on to take the national tests.

End of Key Stage 1 tests

The children are tested in:

- reading
- writing, including spelling and handwriting
- mathematics, including number, shape and space, and measurement
- science.

Year 4 tests

The children are tested in:

- reading
- writing
- spelling
- mathematics.

End of Key Stage 2 tests

The children are tested in:

- English
- mathematics
- science.

These tests are given by the class teacher, but they are sent off to be marked independently, by specially trained markers.

THE RESULTS

You will be told what level your child has reached. The levels are:

- **Level W** – working toward Level 1
- **Level 1** – average for a typical 5-year-old
- **Level 2** – average for a typical 7-year-old
- **Level 3** – average for a typical 9-year-old
- **Level 4** – average for a typical 11-year-old.

   This means that if your child is at Level 2 in the test for the end of Key Stage 1, she's doing as well as you should expect her to. If she's up to Level 3, she's rather ahead. If she's only up to Level 1, then she might need extra help.

HOW TO HELP WITH SATs AT THE END OF YEAR 2

English

Writing

As with previous years, all written work will need to show *correct use of capital letters and full stops*:

- If you have a PC, you could copy a short piece of text from your child's reading book and miss out all the punctuation. Your child could then correct your writing. This could be done with or without the help of the text. A confident child will probably only need the text to check their own corrections!
- If you don't have a PC, or don't want sticky fingers on your keyboard, you could write or print the text out and give your child a red pen to mark your work. The most important thing is to make it fun!

Adjectives and adverbs are always important in written work:

- See how many ways that you can come up with to say 'nice'. Turn it into a game. Describe something as 'nice' and see how many guesses it takes for your child to work out what you actually meant. (Did you mean tasty, attractive, colourful, bright, kind...?)
- Remind your child that adjectives are words that tell us more about things: about objects (for example, a shiny car, a fluffy cat, etc.).
- Tell a really boring story and then together turn into an exciting, funny or scary one. (For example, 'The man walked into the room and sat down on the chair. "What can I do for you?" he said.' This could very easily become – 'The old, poorly clothed man shuffled slowly into the filthy room and sat noisily on the rickety chair. "What can I do for you?" he snarled'.)
- Remind your child that adverbs are words that tell us more about verbs: about actions (for example, the man walked slowly, the rain started suddenly.)

Using a range of connectives is viewed as being the sign of a more advanced write:

- When reading with your child, note how many different words are used. Start with and, move on to but, then see if you can find meanwhile, therefore and because.

Spelling

Marks will be awarded for accuracy, so the more accurate the spelling the higher the spelling level your child will attain. (No surprises there.) *But* by writing down the first letter(s) of a word, a child will get half the marks awarded for spelling! So if your child is not very confident at spelling:

- Play spelling games where all you are looking for is the first letter.
- Play 'I spy'.
- Extend the game by getting your child to write down the first few letters.
- Make up word strings by changing only one letter (for example, cat – hat – hot – hop – top – mop and so on).
- Play a game using 'magic' e – find out how many words you can make by adding an 'e' (for example, hat + e = hate, hop + e = hope, etc.).

With more confident spellers:

- See how many words you can find with a particular spelling blend – the more confident the children are, the more complex the blends you can use.
- Look at a range of words and find out what happens when you add -ing, -ly, -ily, -ed, etc.; remind children of the spelling rules being applied to the words you are looking at.
- Play hangman.
- Make up simple crosswords (you should even be able to buy books with crosswords or word searches in them).

Reading

The main differences between the levels are:

Level 1 looks for *basic word recognition* and being able to read with a degree of *fluency*. The way to help here is to carry on doing all the things you are probably already doing:

- Make sharing a book fun.
- Take it in turns to read aloud from the passage.
- Look at the pictures and use them to help you work out what is going on in the story.
- Split difficult words up by covering the different syllables up with your finger and then sound it out a bit at a time.
- Give lots of smiles and lots of praise.

Level 2 looks for understanding about *plot, setting and characters*. Being able to read long passages or difficult words, although an important step, is not the issue at this level. So if your child is already a fluent reader, you need to:

- Spend less time actually sitting down and listening to them read, but more time talking to them about what is going on in the story.
- Ask questions about the story plot. Then ask the child to show you the parts of the text, that explain what is going on.
- Ask questions about where the story is set. Get the child to find and read out the parts of the text, that describe the setting. (This will also provide a good opportunity to look at adverbs and adjectives.)
- Talk about the characters in the story. Ask questions like, 'How do you think Matilda felt when she was locked in the cupboard?' 'Why do you think Miss Trunchbull treated children as she did?'

Level 3 is assessed by children providing written answers to written questions about a range of texts or varying styles. The children will be given a booklet containing the texts and will then have to write answers, having read the different texts. The main emphasis here will be on *inference*. To attain this level, children will need to be able to 'read between the lines' – that is, to make inferences about things that are not directly stated. Providing help without putting additional pressure on your child will be much harder at this level, given the nature of the assessment. So:

- Ensure that your child is reading both fiction and non-fiction texts.
- Play games along the lines of – 'How quickly can you find out what this book tells us about…?'
- Write down some questions about a text that you have read and ask your child to write out their answers.
- Ask your child to read one page of a text and then ask them questions about it. Make sure that some of your questions require them to make inferences.
- Remember that there are many potential answers to the question, 'How do you think Matilda felt when …'.

Mathematics

Number bonds

Children will be expected to know their number bonds up to 5, 10 and (preferably) 20.

Mental maths games can be played anywhere and at any time, in the car, walking to school, or whilst out shopping in the supermarket. The list is endless. Just remember to make it snappy. Start with easy numbers, make it fun and slowly build up to more complex ones.

Making 5, 10, 20

Ask your child to say what needs to be added to your number to make 5, 10 or 20. The focus is on speed here! Get your child to test you on your speed as well. (They need to have worked out the answer to say whether you are right or wrong.)

What two numbers to make...

Play the same as the game above, except that the child has to come up with two numbers which when added together will then add to your number to make the required total. (For example, making 20, you say 10, they could say 9 + 1, 8 + 2, 7 + 3, etc.)

'If I know ... what do I also know?'

This is simple algebra. If I know that $x + y = z$, then I also know that $y + x = z$, that $z - y = x$ and that $z - x = y$. Say, 'If I know that 7 and 3 make 10, what three other facts do I know?' The child then needs to tell you that 3 and 7 make 10, that 10 take away 7 leaves 3 and that 10 take away 3 leaves 7.

Multiplication tables

The 2×, 5× and 10× multiplication tables must be known:

- start off by chanting the table in its most simple form (for example. '2, 4, 6, 8' ...);
- move on to 'One two is two, two twos are four, three twos are six' ...;
- graduate to random order ('Three twos are six, seven twos are ...?');
- now start all over again using the 5× and 10× tables.
- finally, play the random game using all three multiplication tables at the same time.

Remember, if you know that $3 \times 5 = 15$, then you also know that $5 \times 3 = 15$, that $15 \div 3 = 5$ and that $15 \div 5 = 3$ ($x \times y = z$, therefore $y \times x = z$, etc.).

Going to the shops provides numerous opportunities for mathematics. If one tin of beans costs 'x', then how much will it cost to buy 10? (Reinforce their 2×, 5× and 10× tables' knowledge.)

Estimating

- If pizzas are 99p each, approximately how much will four cost? Don't bother with 99p! Call it £1. Then 4 x £1 = £4. So the pizzas will be about £4.
- So how much, exactly, do I need? The estimate for the pizzas was 1p too high for each of the four pizzas, so I need to take 4p from £4, which will mean the exact cost is £3.96 Try to have some fun and don't worry!

CHAPTER 5

Problems at school

● ● ● ● ● ● ● ● ● ● ● ● ● ● ●

Everyone hopes their child will have a happy and productive time at school. However, sometimes things do go wrong, and when they do, it's important to handle them well in order to minimise their effect. It's also important to realise that sometimes problems can be linked together in complicated ways, and that a problem may have more than one symptom (for instance, behavioural problems may be caused by your child not getting on with the teacher; or underachievement may actually be a sign of a bright child being bored by work that is too easy).

 ## Behavioural problems **www.behaviour.org.uk**

Advice on behavioural problems in children and links to other sites with related information and resources.

BULLYING

Bullying exists in most, if not all, schools. It need not be physical – sometimes bullies intimidate their victims verbally, or even just with looks or body language. Some children who are bullied are also, in their turn, bullies.

All schools should have a policy for dealing with bullying, but applying it means that teachers must recognise that it is going on.

Parents can help a lot here. Remember, a child doesn't have to be out of the ordinary to become a victim or a bully. Changes in a child's normal behaviour are the things to look for.

Signs of victims:

- reluctance to go to school
- arriving at school or home late for no reason
- changing the route to school (especially if the new route is long or inconvenient)
- money or possessions being lost
- requests for extra money (or even stealing from home)
- clothing or possessions being damaged
- moodiness
- bruises, scratches or other signs of fighting
- lack of friends, or loss of friends.

Signs of bullies:

- sudden appearance of extra money or possessions
- major changes in the circle of friends
- sudden dislike of an old friend
- being nasty about one particular child
- attention seeking (for example saying things intended to shock).

Of course, any of these symptoms may have causes other than bullying. It's important to be sure of your facts before you approach the school or anyone else.

Dealing with bullying

Bullying is hard to deal with because any attempt to stop it is likely to make things worse – yet it can't simply be allowed to continue unchecked. It's important to realise that the most desirable outcome is not that the bullies be punished, or even that 'everyone becomes friends', but that the bullying stops.

Strategies that don't work:

- lecturing the bullies
- punishing them

- asking or telling them to be friends
- telling the victim to stick up for themself
- telling him that it will go away if he ignores it
- telling him to change his behaviour.

   Strategies that do work:

- clear and consistent guidelines on bullying
- counselling for victims and bullies
- confronting the bullies with the consequences of their actions.

If you think your child is being bullied:

Do:

- Make sure the school knows what's going on.
- Make sure your child knows she can talk to you (or perhaps to another sympathetic adult).
- Help your child to think and feel positively about herself.
- Consider starting out-of-school activities so your child has a place where she can make other friends.

Don't:

- Blame your child.
- Tell him to stand up for himself.
- Tell him if he ignores it, it will stop.

Bullying www.bullying.co.uk

Children who are being bullied can get advice online here. For the parents of children who are being bullied, there are model letters – send one of these in to school, and it won't be ignored. And there are problem pages – the advice is helpful and they will help you to feel less isolated.

Bullying Online

Children:
Help and advice for children who are having a hard time at school. Information on how to stay safe.

Parents:
Help and advice for parents who are tackling bullying. Don't forget!! you can always email us for more help or advice.

Legal:
Advice from a solicitor & model letters for you to send to your school which cannot be ignored.

School Projects
help with those all important projects. Amaze your classmates and baffle your teachers.

Problem page for Pupils
Sometimes you think you're the only one with problems but you're not.

Problem page for Parents
Dealing with bullying can be very isolating for a parent.

Contacts & Requests
The best people to talk to on specific issues and our requests for help.

Access to pupil records
Advice if you are denied your right to a copy of your child's school file.

A Governor's Advice
A governor's advice to governor's and parents.

Sample Letters
Sample letters that you can send to your school.

What People Say
The kind words that people have said about Bullying Online.

Outside School
Bullying happens outside school as well.

Bullying policies
Tell us about the bullying policies which work — and those which don't

Tips
Have you got any tips for pupils being bullied? We can put them on our website.

Guidelines
The bullying guidelines issued by the National Association of Head Teachers.

Help Others
Are you an older bullying victim? Would you like to contact others who have had the same experience?

Sponsorship
Running Bullying Online is very expensive. Help our work by becoming a sponsor.

A B C
Anti Bullying Campaign

Bullying Online & The Anti Bullying Campaign.
We've joined forces with the London based Anti Bullying Campaign. This will enable more people to get advice more quickly. You can contact The Anti Bullying Campaign on **0171 378 1446**

Email Bullying Online
The site is open 24 hours a day, 365 days a year. Contact us on help@bullying.co.uk

Creators of Bullying Online

23012 WebTracker

National Society for the Prevention of Cruelty to Children **www.nspcc.org.uk**

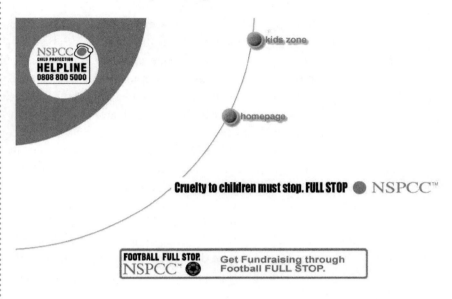

This site gives the NSPCC's views on bullying, including information about its education programme which has several useful ideas to combat bullying. There is also have a freephone advice line for children and carers – 0800 800 500.

EARLY PROBLEMS

Many children have difficulty settling in when they first start in the reception class. They may be upset at being separated from their parents and their familiar environment, and at having to meet a crowd of new people, many of whom behave in unfamiliar ways.

Problems in the first few days or weeks at school are nothing to worry about too much. Remember that all this might be new to you and your child, but the teachers are used to helping children get used to school. Good teachers won't embarrass or humiliate your child (or you), but will help you find ways round the problems.

Problems might include:

- **Not wanting to use the toilet** – some children just don't like using 'public' toilets, either because they are embarrassed or because they are scared they can't cope. You can help by making sure your child knows how to use the toilet (for example, what a chain, lever and push button flush look like), and can put his clothes back together afterwards. You might also try taking your child to use the public toilets in places like cinemas and shopping centres. If your child is just forgetful (for instance, because they get so involved in what they are doing) a system of rewards for staying clean might help. But don't reverse this and punish your child for having accidents.

- **Not wanting to eat lunch** – again, some children are just shy about eating in public; or they may find the noise and activity of a big lunch hall difficult to cope with; or they may be picky about what they will eat. Some schools help with this by setting aside a special area for the reception class to have lunch. Your child will never be forced to eat, but she will be gently encouraged. You should inform the school of any special dietary requirements (for example, because of medical conditions or religious restrictions) and tell your child that you have done so.

- **Difficulty concentrating, especially at story time** – it can be difficult for young children to concentrate for long periods of time. This is a skill they can build up over time, with the teacher's help. You can help too, by reading with your child, playing number games and so on. For more ideas, *see* Chapter 7 on homework.

- **Refusing to do what they are told** – some children don't understand that they must do what the teacher tells them. Others may try to test their boundaries by being naughty or disobedient. It's important that you back the teacher up, providing consistency between the home and school, and that both you and the teacher correct bad behaviour gently but firmly.

- **Having a hard time sharing or making friends** – some children find it difficult to make friends or share with others. Ideally, you will have helped your child by taking him to a playgroup before school started, or introduced him to other children in similar settings. If not, and you do have this problem at school, try inviting one or two children round to play at weekends. Another idea is to join up for after-school activities such as gym classes, sports or Brownies.

- **Stealing** – your child may not realise that the things in the classroom aren't hers to keep. If she does bring things home, just explain this to her and get her to take them back next day. If she brings home another child's belongings, you will probably want her to apologise; this should be done without embarrassing or humiliating your child.

Reception-class teachers are used to these problems. If you are worried, make a time to go and talk to your child's teacher about whatever's on your mind. The chances are, that the teacher will be able to reassure you and perhaps suggest ways you can help.

If the problem persists past the first few weeks, or if it seems to be getting worse (or if new problems keep arising) then you should go and talk to the teacher again and see if more help is needed.

PROBLEMS LATER ON

Problems later in a child's school career fall roughly into two types – on-going problems (those which the child always seems to have), and sudden-onset problems (caused by a change of circumstance, for instance).

On-going problems

It can be difficult for a parent – or a school – to admit it, but some children do have more difficulty with school life than others. They may find it hard to accept authority, or to become interested in their work; or they may not see the long-term value in gaining an education.

If your child is having on-going problems at school:

Do:

- Keep in contact with the school.
- Try to identify possible underlying causes and discuss what can be done about them with the school.
- Try to keep an open mind (don't go in with all guns blazing in defence of your child; on the other hand, don't assume she must automatically be in the wrong in all situations).

- Make sure your child continues to attend school every day, all day.
- Try to maintain consistency between the home and school environments (for example, if rudeness is wrong at school, then it is also wrong at home).
- Make sure your child understands the consequences of what he is doing (for example, a good school policy will explain what happens if children persistently break the rules).
- Set rules at home and make sure your child sticks to them (it can be a good idea to discuss what they should be with your child – and what should happen if they are broken).
- Provide opportunities for your child to achieve outside school, both in informal and formal situations.
- Be open to the idea that your child's behaviour is improving, and make sure her teacher notices it too.
- Praise good behaviour.

If problems continue, or get worse, you might want to ask the school about what additional help (such as counselling or extra support in class) is available.

Don't:

- Assume your child is being made a scapegoat.
- Be aggressive with teachers and other school staff.
- Assume the situation can't be changed.

Sudden-onset problems

Some children run into difficulties because of a change in circumstance. Some examples might include:

- parents divorcing or separating
- parent remarrying
- parents or carers losing job
- bereavement
- moving
- onset of puberty.

If any of these problems – or others like them – occur, it's doubly important to make sure the school knows what is going on. Most teachers will make allowances when children are having a bad time through no fault of their own. It's also increasingly common for schools to provide counselling, especially in cases such as bereavement or divorce; or they may be able to direct you to getting your child help outside school.

Divorce Recovery Workshop, DRW **www.drw.org.uk**

DRW is a UK-wide self-help group run by volunteers who have attended its workshop. There are no 'experts' but all those involved will have personally experienced a relationship break-up.

SPECIAL EDUCATIONAL NEEDS

If your child is severely disruptive or troubled emotionally, the school may decide that he has special needs. Many children have occasional problems with specific pieces of work, or find some subjects easier or more fun than others. Sometimes these problems sort themselves out in a short period of time. If they don't, the school should provide extra help.

Other children get so far behind with their work, or develop such severe behaviour problems that they stop learning themselves and disrupt the rest of the class.

Some problems are obvious even before the child goes to school – for example, the child may have Down's syndrome, or be autistic, or have a physical disability such as blindness or deafness.

Down Syndrome Educational Trust **www.downsnet.org/downsed**

The Down Syndrome Educational Trust is a charitable company, registered in England and Wales. It was founded in 1996 to continue and develop the work of the Portsmouth Down Syndrome Trust.

Down syndrome community **www.downscity.com**

This American site is intended to provide a forum for information affecting the Down syndrome community and to maximize use of the internet by any and all members of the Down syndrome community.

These children can be placed on the Special Needs Register maintained by all schools. Eventually, they may be given a Statement of Special Educational Need (often just referred to as 'statementing'), ensuring that they get the highest level of extra help.

It can be difficult for parents to admit their children have problems, but being placed on the SEN Register is quite often the best way to get extra help. So, although it can be tempting to argue against it, that's very often not the best thing to do.

You'll often hear teachers talking about a child 'being SEN' if they are on the Register. Reasons for placing a child on the Register include:

- underachieving (usually if children are two years behind in a key area like reading, they are considered to be SEN)
- severe emotional difficulties and/or severely disruptive behaviour
- autism
- dyslexia
- attention deficit hyperactivity disorder (ADHD)
- physical impairment (deafness, blindness etc.).

National Autistic Society **www.oneworld.org/autism_uk**

NAS is a UK organisation for people with autism and those who care for them, spearheading national and international initiatives and providing a strong voice for autism. The organisation works in many areas to help people with autism live their lives with as much independence as possible.

British Dyslexics **www.dyslexia.uk.com**

Many parents will have concerns over dyslexia. Fortunately for most the symptoms are fairly minor and often disappear with time. British Dyslexics is a charity devoted to helping all children, regardless of their background and the ability of their parents to pay. The site offers useful background information, symptoms and suggestions. There are also useful contacts for other organisations that may be able to help. Finally, attention deficit hyperactivity disorder (ADHD) is briefly covered.

About Dyslexia

Assessments

Attention Deficit Disorder.

Bullying

Charity Profile

Children that we Help

Coming to terms with SEN

Dyslexia Gene

Dyslexia Updates

Education

Famous Dyslexics

Importance of IQ

Index of LEA's

FREE INFORMATION PACK
Ring us during office hours
Tel: 01244 815552 / 822884 / 816683

Our charity is distinctly different from the British Dyslexia Association and the Dyslexia Institute. We are not only interested in helping children and teenagers to succeed in both compulsory, further and higher education, but we also passionately believe that getting extra help should not depend on a parents ability to pay for extra tuition. Unlike the British Dyslexia Association or the Dyslexia Institute we make *no charges* for any of the services or information we provide.

ADHD www.angelfire.com/wv/wetzel/index5.html

A collection of links to ADHD information and resources.

Royal National Institute for the Blind www.rnib.org.uk

RNIB is one of the UK's biggest and most diverse charities. It provides over 60 different services for almost a million people with serious sight problems throughout the country.

Royal National Institute for Deaf People
www.rnid.org.uk

RNID's vision is a world where deafness and hearing loss are not barriers to opportunity and fulfilment.

National Deaf Children's Society www.ndcs.org.uk

NDCS is a UK charity exclusively dedicated to supporting all deaf children, young deaf people and their families in overcoming the challenges of childhood deafness.

How a child gets given a statement of special educational need

This is a gradual process and can end at any stage. Before the school considers putting your child on the Register, they will talk to you about the problems they feel your child is having. It's important that you find out exactly what these are and that you get a chance to have your say about them. Ideally, you will agree a plan of action with the school. You will probably be introduced to the Special Needs Co-ordinator – the specialist within the school who is responsible for SEN provision.

If it is decided that your child should go on the Register, a teacher will explain the school's Special Needs Code of Practice – all schools have one, and it goes into detail about the kinds of help that are available, and the way your child's progress will be monitored.

There are five stages of Special Need, providing different levels of extra help.

Stage 1

The child gets extra help in class from the class teacher, generally with advice from the Special Needs Co-ordinator. Between them, the teachers will make sure that your child is given the appropriate help and that she is assessed at intervals to see if the problems have been sorted out, or whether she needs to move on to Stage 2.

Stage 2

More help is needed, which is often provided by the school's Special Needs Co-ordinator, working with children in small groups. At this stage, your child will be given an Individual Education Plan. This is specially devised for your child; it breaks her work down into small steps and sets precise targets. The idea is to enable the teachers to monitor your child exactly. Also, by giving the child small, achievable goals, her confidence is kept as high as possible.

Stage 3

A specialist teacher from outside the school provides extra help (perhaps teaching small groups or individuals). For example, the school may decide that your child needs a specialist dyslexia teacher. Again, her progress will be closely monitored.

Stage 4

The child is assessed to see if it is appropriate to give her a Statement of Special Needs. Most children get all the help they need at Stages 1, 2 or 3. However, some children need more help than the school can provide out of their normal resources and this can be provided by giving the child a Statement.

If you think your child would be helped by being Statemented, you can ask the school to move her on to Stage 4. If they don't want to, and you still think it would be appropriate, you can approach the LEA.

Once everyone has agreed that your child should be assessed, tests will be carried out by the school, by an educational psychologist, and by other appropriate specialists (for example, speech therapist, doctor).

Stage 5 – the child is given a Statement

If the assessment shows that your child does need more help than can be provided by Stage 3 of the Code of Practice, she will be given a Statement of Special Needs. This sets out exactly what problems your child is having, and what help is needed.

It is unlikely (but possible) that your child will be given a place in a Special School. Another option is to place children in a unit attached to a mainstream school. Either one will have expertise in the particular kind of difficulty your child is experiencing. However, current practice is to include as many children in mainstream schooling as possible, so it is likely that extra help will be given in your child's school. This may include help from extra staff or equipment in class (such as computer equipment – for example, voice recognition software, specially adapted toilets or changing facilities).

Points to remember if your child has special needs

Do:

- Keep in close contact with the school.
- Make sure you see copies of reports and assessments, and get explanations of anything that is unclear; you can comment on them at various stages.
- Do what you can to speed up the statementing process by asking questions and making sure that the school has all the information it needs.
- Be prepared to fight if you think a bad decision is being made (for example, if your child is assigned a place in a Special School, but you think mainstream education would be more appropriate, or vice versa; or to get specialist help or equipment).
- Be aware that you can go with your child to meet specialists like the educational psychologist or the speech therapist.

If you are completely unhappy with the result of the assessment, you can appeal to the SEN Tribunal. Ask the LEA or the Citizen's Advice Bureau how to do this – but move as quickly as you can, since there is a time limit.

W W W British Stammering Association www.stammering.org

Many children will stammer at some time, but often this is just a temporary state, perhaps even affected by something like a bad cold. This site includes a lot of background information on stammering, including some example conversations to have with your child to try and help the situation.

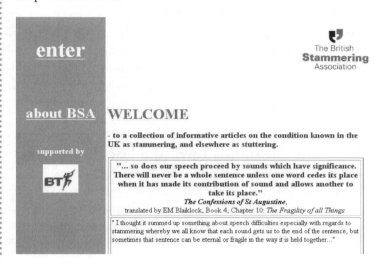

UNDERACHIEVING

Not all children who underachieve in school have Special Needs. Other causes might include:

- a bright child being bored by work that is too easy;
- a difficulty with a particular subject (perhaps caused by the child losing confidence);
- discipline problems having a knock-on effect on work;
- conflicts with the teacher;
- poor teaching.

A bright child being bored by work that is too easy

It does sometimes happen that bright children become bored and disruptive if they are not stretched by the work they are given. If the teacher does not notice, it may be up to you, the parent or carer, to point this out. This problem may crop up when your child changes teacher, or if the class has a period with a supply teacher because the regular teacher is away.

A difficulty with a particular subject

Children are just as likely as adults to have subjects they enjoy and are good at – and ones which they don't like, or have problems with. The main thing is not to let the child lose confidence in his ability at other subjects, or to feel that he'll never catch up. There may be ways you can help your child at home, but this may not be wise if it just causes additional stress

Discipline problems having a knock-on effect on work

If your child is finding it difficult to cope with the discipline of going to school, the chances are that this will also affect her work. The best strategy here is probably to deal with the underlying causes of the discipline problems, while doing what you can to keep your child's confidence in her abilities up.

This is a bit of a chicken and egg situation, but very often a child who finds something she is good at will settle down and be less disruptive – and a child who is less disruptive is more likely to work well. So an approach that looks at all sides of the problem is the most likely to succeed.

Conflicts with the teacher

As in any group situation, personality conflicts sometimes arise in classrooms. Most teachers try very hard not to have favourites, or at least not to let their preferences show. But with the best will in the world, sometimes they do. If you seriously think your child is having conflicts with the teacher that are not caused by simple naughtiness or disruptive behaviour, you should talk to the school about it – starting with your child's teacher, but perhaps involving the headteacher as well. If you feel your child can cope with it, you might suggest that she is involved in the discussion.

With luck, once the problem has been discussed, it will become easier for your child to cope with – especially if the teacher is confident enough and sensitive enough to see the problem without being threatened by it. You are most likely to get the result you want if you can try to see both sides of the problem – even though you may feel that the teacher (as the adult) should be the one to change.

If it can't be resolved this way, in a larger school transferring to another class might be a possibility (though very much a last resort). In small schools with only one class per year, it won't be. In that case, all you can really do is support your child until he changes class at the end of the year, while continuing to make the school aware of the problem.

In some schools, teachers move up with their classes. A great deal of office politics surrounds the allocation of classes to teachers in most schools, so you should make sure the headteacher is aware that you will have a problem if your child is made to stay with a teacher with whom they really don't get on. You might even want to approach the governors (particularly the parent governors) and explain your problem. However, you should also be aware that the headteacher is trying to fit a complicated jigsaw together and so may not be able to find a solution that suits everyone.

Poor teaching

The introduction of OFSTED inspections, the National Curriculum and other government initiatives, should, in theory, have eliminated most really bad teaching. However, it is possible that your child's teacher is having problems.

Your first action should probably be to talk to the teacher, though tact may be required. It may be, for example, that the teacher is using a method you aren't familiar with – and if your child hasn't quite understood it, it can be quite easy to think they are being badly taught. You should also be very careful that you aren't trying to avoid the idea that your child may have learning difficulties or need extra support.

If you are sure, and talking to the teacher doesn't allay your fears, then you should make an appointment to see the headteacher.

CHAPTER 6

Getting involved with your child's school

● ● ● ● ● ● ● ● ● ● ● ● ●

One of the best ways of helping your child's education is to get actively involved with the school. This will give you the opportunity to find out more about what happens at school, and also staff and teachers will get to know you and your family.

HOME–SCHOOL AGREEMENT

Starting in September 1999, every school introduced a Home–School Agreement, which all parents or adults responsible for a child will have to sign. This is a contract between you and your child's school. The school should have written it in consultation with the parents, so it shouldn't hold many surprises. The agreements will vary from school to school, but they will probably cover such matters as:

- standards of teaching and achievement
- attendance and punctuality
- behaviour
- homework
- uniform or dress code
- the ethos or spirit of the school.

You will be expected to sign the Agreement to say that you understand it and agree to be bound by its terms. Older children may also be asked to sign it. If you or your child break the Agreement, you will probably be asked in to talk about it with the headteacher. In serious cases, your child may be disciplined or excluded from school.

Parents' Centre **www.parents.dfee.gov.uk**

This is the official parents' site of the DfEE. The site is usefully split into two key sections: in school and out of school. The first covers all the key aspects of schools, with much of the official documentation. For example, is it is possible to find the official line on school uniforms and school meals. This background information can be very useful if you need to discuss any issues with your school. The out-of-school section provides plenty of links for helping at home with suggestions of things to do. It also covers the official details on Home–School Agreements.

VOLUNTEERING

Many schools welcome volunteers. One important way parents can help is with fundraising, which is normally done through the Parent–Teacher Association. However, you might also be able to volunteer to:

- help in class (for instance, by listening to children read)
- go on class outings
- sort library books
- help with costumes for school plays
- help at school sports days and fêtes and with fundraising activities (you'll find some ideas about this on page 113.

Getting started as a volunteer

Ask your child's teacher or the school secretary how you can help. Remember to mention any relevant skills or experience you have – and do tell them what you'd like to be involved in!

Expect the school to check your background – by law, anyone in school who has regular contact with children must be checked against 'List 99' – a list of everyone in the country who has been banned from working with young people. You will need to provide your full name and date of birth.

Do:

- Make a commitment you can keep, and let the teacher know in advance if you can't make it.
- Treat the children the way you would like your own child to be treated.
- Ask for advice or help from the teacher if you need it.
- Find out the rules of the school and the class – and make sure the children know you know.
- Set an example.
- Enjoy yourself – the children will pick up on it!

Don't:

- Necessarily expect to work in your child's class – it may be against school policy, and it may not be for the best anyway.
- Over-commit yourself, especially at first.
- Just turn up and expect to be able to fit in – the teacher needs to be able to plan her lessons with your help in mind.
- Shout at, be rude to, or (especially) hit the children.
- Gossip about the children to other parents.

THE PARENT–TEACHER ASSOCIATION

Some Parent–Teacher Associations are informal – little more than a group of volunteers who get together to do fundraising and find people to help out in school. Other schools have Associations that are formally organised, and which are usually affiliated to the Confederation of Parent–Teacher Associations. These will have a committee made up of officers (secretary, treasurer and chairperson) and ordinary members. The school staff may be represented as well (the headteacher, for instance, may be the president).

The parents of all the children in the school are automatically members of the Association and can put themselves forward to join the committee. The committee decides what to do and when to do it. Many events will be fundraisers (for example, jumble sales, raffles, car-boot sales). Others may be social and to raise morale (for example, firework displays, dances).

W
W
W

National Confederation of Parent–Teacher Associations
www.ncpta.org.uk

NCPTA represents more than 6 million parents and teachers through more than 11,000 member associations. NCPTA promotes partnerships between home and school; pupils, parents, carers and teachers; parents and LEAs and other interested organisations. The site provides details of what the NCPTA does and outlines its aims and objectives. National, regional and area contact details can be obtained, and you can apply online for a form to join the NCPTA. As a member of NCPTA, you will receive the magazine *Home and School* containing articles of topical interest, book reviews, equipment news and special offers and also regular newsletters.

BECOMING A GOVERNOR

All state schools have a governing body. The number of governors depends on the size of the school. The governing body includes:

- two elected parents of children at the school
- one elected teacher
- co-opted governors from the local business community
- appointed governors from the LEA (who may or may not be councillors)
- for church schools, representatives of the church foundation.

The governors:

- see to staffing the school (numbers of staff, appointments, promotions, discipline)
- allocate spending within the budget they are given by the LEA
- decide on the ethos of the school and find ways to promote it
- work out a development plan for the school
- draw up the Action Plan that must be implemented after an OFSTED inspection.

How to become a governor

You should really only think about becoming a governor if you have the best interests of the whole school in mind. It isn't really enough just to be worried about your own child – or for that matter, the interests of your own political party or religion.

There are several ways to become a governor. You can be:

- **Elected as a parent governor** – the school will let you know when elections are due; all parents over 18 can stand for election, and they all have a vote.
- **Appointed by the local authority** – not all LEA governors are councillors. Many are ordinary people appointed because there are not enough councillors for all the schools. Contact your local authority and ask if they have a list of people who wish to be school governors that you could join.
- **Co-opted by the governing body** – write to the governors explaining your interest. When there is a vacancy, they may contact you. The government is especially interested in getting more local business people on to the governing bodies of schools.
- **A foundation governor** – if you are interested in a church school, contact the officials of your local church to see if this is a possibility.

FUNDRAISING

Fundraising is a perennial problem for most schools. Even if they're lucky enough to have enough money for all their basic needs, there are always extras it would be good to have. It can also be a great way to boost morale, get parents, staff and children working together, and forge links with the wider community.

The range of things you can do to raise cash is limited only by your imagination – though of course it's a good idea to check out the legal situation and to make sure everything is done safely. You may also need insurance if you run events. If you're in any doubt, phone your local Trading Standards Authority or try your local council.

WWW

UK fundraising **www.fundraising.co.uk**

This is a big resources site for all those involved in fundraising, including sources of funding, guidelines on writing applications and plenty of examples. Although mainly aimed at charities, there is plenty here that would be of interest to schools.

There are a number of ways to make the most of a good idea:

- Start planning early.
- The more outrageous and imaginative the idea, the more likely it is to capture people's attention (and wallets); but before you commit yourselves, delegate a couple of people to research how feasible it is (whether it'll need much seed money to get started; those legal and safety concerns mentioned above; insurance; whether or not you'll need outside help and how easy it'll be to get it).
- Publicise your event well – not just in the school, but in the local community too. Think about fliers and posters, but consider contacting the local paper and perhaps even local radio.
- If you're going to need any kind of professional help, find it early on. Hope for sponsorship, but plan on paying if you have to – after you've assessed whether it's going to be worth it.
- Concentrate your efforts – lots of little events may just end up trying people's patience, whereas a couple of big ones could fire their enthusiasm.

- You may get a better response if the fundraising is for a specific purpose (for instance, to redecorate the nursery, or to buy books for the junior library) instead of just adding to general funds.
- Vary what you do – that 'not again' feeling won't raise morale or cash.
- Make sure your ideas really are fun and will appeal to a lot of people (sponsored bus spotting, for instance, is likely to be a niche activity...).
- Make sure you have enough volunteers – both while you're preparing, and on the day – and make sure they know what they're doing. Be prepared to delegate, but have back-up plans in case anyone lets you down.
- There's bound to be stress at times, but try to make sure everyone feels valued. Blood on the carpet doesn't raise money and may leave you short of volunteers for next time.

Fundraising ideas break down into a few basic categories: collecting things, sponsorship and events.

Collecting things

Take part in one (or all) of the schemes run by super-markets, newspapers and manufacturers for people to collect till receipts. Put collecting boxes near the main entrance, or ask teachers to collect them from the children at registration.

Collect cans, tin foil, and used stamps to sell. Many of the well-known retail and consumer companies operate reward schemes for schools, whereby you collect vouchers when shopping. These can then be redeemed by your school for certain equipment. For example, look at Tescos Computers for School scheme (**www.tesco.com/ computersforschools**). Other schemes can be found at **www.parents.org.uk**

Sponsorship

There are two kinds of sponsorship – getting people to raise money by being sponsored, and getting businesses to sponsor something the school needs.

Children can be sponsored for reading, walking (round the play-ground if you can't take them out somewhere more interesting), picking up litter, or for keeping silent. Adults can be sponsored for dieting, giving up smoking, or not swearing (put a swear box in the staff room – if you dare).

The kind of business sponsorship you can find depends on what the school needs. Some possibilities are listed below, but you may want to bear in mind that some people dislike the idea of too close a rela-tionship between businesses and schools. Things to be aware of are the appropriateness of the business (few people are likely to be com-fortable with the idea of cigarette companies paying for schoolbooks, for example), the quality of what they provide, and what they'll want in return. As long as everyone's happy, you could consider asking local or national companies about:

- providing or paying for schoolbooks, computers, or sports equipment;
- teaching packs (which should be vetted for bias);
- renovations and maintenance for specific parts of the school;
- prizes and equipment for fundraising events.

Events

Imagination is the only thing limiting the kind of events you can run – though some will be more lucrative and easier to run than others. Although some ideas, like jumble sales and car-boot fairs, can be run at any time, it's a nice idea to tie some fundraisers in with events and celebrations around the year. For example:

Autumn Term:

- **Harvest Festival** – sell home-made cakes, jams, and donated canned food and plants.
- **Hallowe'en** – oragnise a Monster Mash disco (for children and/or adults) – themed, with prizes for the creepiest costume and the most monstrous make up. Sell food – you'll find lots of gruesome recipes on the Parents Online website (**www.parents.org.uk**); have a Jack

o' lantern competition (see if you can get a local greengrocer to donate pumpkins).

- **Guy Fawkes Night** – hold a bonfire party, and sell themed food, (bear in mind this needs a lot of attention to safety).
- **Christmas** – hold a Frost Fair – contact local crafts people and invite them to sell their goods (charge a fee per table – easier to administer than charging commission); sell cards and crafts made by the children; make a Santa's Grotto and charge for visits – get local businesses to donate toys for gifts, and find someone with an instant camera to take photos of the children with Father Christmas; sell homemade cakes, preserves; make up bowls of bulbs timed to flower at Christmas, such as narcissi and hyacinths; sell snacks and warm drinks, such as alcohol-free 'mulled wine' (you'll need a licence to sell the real thing); stage a Christmas Panto – the sillier the better, and if you make it really outrageous, you should be able to get coverage by the local papers.

Spring Term:

- **Valentine's Day** – make and sell cards, plant cuttings, and bouquets of paper flowers; hold a themed Valentine's Day disco; raffle a bottle of champagne; run a 'Mr and Mrs' style quiz.
- **Shrove Tuesday** – hold a Pancake Party – and have a competition for the 'best flipper'. Or hold a pancake race (see **www.parents.org.uk** for pancake recipes).
- **Mother's Day** – yet another chance to sell cards, cakes and flowers.
- **Easter** – spring barbecue – sell food and drink; make hats and have an Easter Bonnet parade; don't forget to make a simnel cake; hold a fashion show – some national clothing companies will run these for schools.

Summer Term:

- **School sports day** – probably more of a morale raiser than an opportunity to raise cash, but you could still sell food and lay on a few small events, like face painting; and don't forget to have silly races for the parents (three-legged race, anyone?).

- **Summer fête** – there are masses of things you can do as part of a summer fête – some of them are easy and cheap to run; others require more organisation, or need a bit of cash to get started. Before you turn to commercial hire companies, don't forget to check out the local council and charities to see what they have on offer. One good hint is to have timed events through the afternoon, such as raffle draws and competition judging, so that people have a reason to hang around.

- **Things to sell** – home-made cakes, jam, sweets; plant cuttings; bric-a-brac; clothes (probably best not to let it get too jumble sale-ish – try keeping things on racks instead of just on a table); books and old magazines; jewellery; painted/decorated plantpots; crafts – get local crafts people along, and charge them a per-table fee; toys; donated food (beware anything that may go off, or that needs refrigeration); food – think sandwiches and cold drinks as well as tea and coffee; but also consider a barbecue. Have somewhere for people to sit – they'll stay longer; candyfloss (hire a machine); ice cream; canned drinks.

- **Competitions**; raffle (check with your local Trading Standards Authority about the legal side of things); 'How many sweets in the jar?' competition; 'Guess the weight of the cake' competition; fancy dress; best/biggest vegetable, cake, etc.; dog with the waggiest tail, sweetest face, etc. (you could even consider having a whole pet show!); the 'Pound in the Bucket' game – fill a bucket with water and put a pound coin at the bottom, then anyone who can drop in a 2p piece so the pound is completely covered gets to keep it – otherwise they lose their 2p (very easy to organise and surprisingly lucrative); tombola; whacky races – anything that involves people making a fool of themselves is likely to draw a crowd …

- **Sideshows**; facepainting; hat making (you could have a parade/competition at the end); fortune telling (get someone to dress up as 'Gypsy Rose Lee' or 'Madame Arcana' – just make sure everyone knows it's only for fun); bouncy castle or bungee run (you may need to hire these – you'll need to decide if you can make the money back from them, or whether they're worth it as a loss-leader); Aunt Sally – paint funny figures on plywood with holes for people to put their faces through, then charge for the chance to pelt them with wet sponges …; coconut shy (hire it); other hired funfair sideshows, from roundabouts to shooting galleries – though it's also possible to have fun making your own (try making a hoop-la stall by painting up old wine boxes); crockery crash – people pay to release their aggression by hurling old china at a wall (take care over safety with this idea).

Events to run at any time of the year

- **Car-boot fairs** – possibly the exception to the rule of not repeating yourselves too often: car-boot fairs attract regular visitors, so if you have the stamina and the parent-power you could easily run one a month.
- **Auctions** – ideal for selling big donated items. However, you may also be able to persuade local restaurants to give away meals – or try for cinema and theatre tickets, or tickets for sporting events. Autographs sometimes do well (especially if you can get something like a football signed by the whole local squad). You can also auction services, such as babysitting or decorating services (the fee goes to the school – the buyer may or may not get a huge bargain and the giver has given time and skills rather than money or goods). It's worth finding a professional auctioneer, or at least an experienced amateur.
- **Jumble sales** – good for selling off donations that didn't sell (or weren't quite up to standard) at the school fête. Don't forget to make extra cash by selling refreshments.
- **Quiz nights** – these can be themed or general. People get together in teams, and there's an entry fee. Sit each team at their own table, and provide a bottle of wine and some snacks or perhaps bread and cheese. The entry fees cover your costs, but you can make more money by selling drinks and food. Do make sure you have enough questions! (See **http://dspace.dial.pipex.com/mcinroy/directory.htm** for a source of questions on all kinds of trivia.)
- **Murder mystery** – find a company that usually runs these at hotels around the country and see if they can do an afternoon/evening one at your school – there may be a limit on how many people they can handle, though.

Murder-mystery events **www.moriarty.co.uk**

Murder-mystery events throughout the UK entertaining at hotels, restaurants, private parties, etc.

Events **www.mayhem.org.uk**

Murder-mystery events, separate murder scripts, treasure hunts, themed dinners, corporate hospitality, team-building events, evening entertainment and dinner theatre.

Links

For more information, look up these links:

General leisure information:

- **www.tradingstandards.gov.uk/schools** (to find your local office)
- **www.charity-commission.gov.uk/cc49.htm**
- **www.ecd-online.co.uk/sections/support.htm**
- **www.neige.freeserve.co.uk** (charity work and fundraising)
- **www.parents-news.co.uk**
- **www.scoutbase.org.uk/inter/jambo/moot/erttmf.htm** (aimed at Scouts, but has a huge list of ideas and fundraising information)
- **www.recycle.mcmail.com/cans.htm** (collect cans and foil and sell it)
- **www.cosmic.org.uk/ptadevon/helpptas.htm#funds** (great site for PTAs; based in Devon, but generally applicable)
- **www.eig.org.uk/fws** (fireworks code sponsored by Black Cat Fireworks)
- **www.fire.org.uk/firework/home.htm** (official Fire Service site)

Hire firms

- **www.funfair.ndirect.co.uk/links.html**
- **www.hinchbk.cambs.sch.uk/feast/feasthome.html**
- **www.inflatable.co.uk/direct.html**
- **www.leisure-hire.co.uk/entertainment.htm**
- **www.tentaprises.co.uk**
- **www.tlgleisure.co.uk/castles_1.htm**
- **www.unclebrian.co.uk** (entertainers, inflatables, etc. for hire)
- **www.allgood.demon.co.uk/Default1.htm** (organise race nights)

CHAPTER 7

Helping your child at home

● ● ● ●

There are plenty of things that you can do to help your child at home. Even children as young as four can expect homework, so in this section you'll find information on how to help generally and with specific subject areas.

HOMEWORK

There are lots of ways you can help with homework – without actually providing your child with the answers! Of course, you can help with specific pieces of work (for instance, by suggesting where to look something up), but there are ways to help more generally too.

Homework High **www.homeworkhigh.com**

These days, almost as soon as they start primary school most children will get an element of homework. Since today's teaching methods are often different to that experienced by the majority of parents, any available help for parents can be invaluable. Homework High is an ambitious project from Channel 4 that aims to help you and your children with homework. The site covers years 1 to 11, although not surprisingly most of the activity is at the upper age range. It is possible to submit your own questions to a panel of qualified teachers. There is also a massive and growing database of previously answered questions.

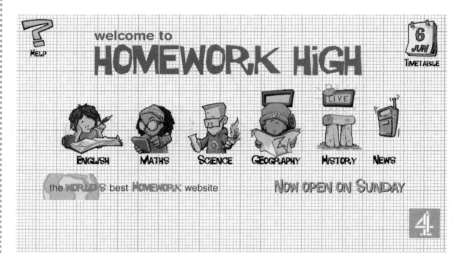

Homework guidelines

Homework is so essential to your child's education that the government has laid down new guidelines about it. These cover the amount that should be set and what it should cover:

- **Years 1 and 2** – one hour a week, covering reading, spelling other literacy work; also number work.
- **Years 3 and 4** – one and a half hours per week, covering numeracy and literacy, and occasionally other subjects.
- **Year 5 and 6** – thirty minutes per day, with a regular timetable; literacy and numeracy continue to be emphasised, but the work ranges over the other subjects too.

However, homework should not replace other after-school activities, such as sport, music and organised activities like Brownies and Cubs.

It is important that your child knows you think homework is important, and that it should be done well. On the other hand, there's no point doing the work for your child, or getting so worried about it that your child gets upset about it.

Do:

- Make sure your child knows you think homework is important, but that she can approach you with any problems.
- Provide a comfortable, quiet place to work.
- Encourage some kind of routine with homework.
- Provide the right equipment (but fancy stationery isn't necessary, no matter what your child says!).
- Remember to praise your child for completed homework.

Don't:

- Just tell your child the answer to a problem – give guidance as to how to work it out or where to find it out instead.
- Make your child copy answers out until they are perfect – seeing your child's mistakes helps your child's teacher know what kind of guidance to give next.

Learnfree www.learnfree.co.uk

This site is intended to provide a range of free support relevant to all stages of the educational process from pre-school to 16+. Look here for information on practical, fun, activities you can do at home to give your child a head start in life – and happy memories to share. You'll also find help through the maze of finding the best education and childcare, tips on starting school, and much more. Learnfree Primary aims to help you support your child's learning at home, and understand how he's progressing at school. Help is available to assist in choosing the best school for your child, advice on common problems, and updates on educational news and research.

STUDY SKILLS

These are general skills used in most subjects. Obviously, the older your child is, the more sophisticated the skills she will be able to use. For example:

- Organising (the place your child works at, the equipment she uses, making sure he has everything for school the next day).
- Using pens, pencils, rubbers, pencil sharpeners, and rulers appropriately.
- Concentrating on reading or a piece of work.
- Reading skills (such as reading silently and understanding the meaning; using contents pages, indexes, dictionaries and encyclopaedias; knowing the difference between a fact and an opinion; being able to draw conclusions from the information she is given).
- Writing skills (organising material; taking notes; planning a story or essay; evaluating it; being able to change it to make it better).

Build a desk unit for your child, perhaps making it a family project.

Reading

- Always keep reading enjoyable.
- Remember that not all reading has to stretch the child.
- Let your child choose her own reading material, and don't criticise it.
- Let your child see you reading, so she knows you think it is important.
- Join the library.

With younger children

- Find a calm, comfortable place to read together. Help your child understand how books work – which way round they go, that the print runs from left to right and so on.
- Choose different kinds of material (stories, factual books, comics) and don't be surprised if your child wants to read the same book again and again. He'll move on when he's ready.
- Don't worry if your child wants to 'tell you the story' but then what he 'reads' doesn't match the words on the page. This is a valuable pre-reading activity.

- Help your child to understand the story by talking about the pictures, the plot and characters.
- Look for patterns such as repeated first letters or sounds, rhymes, or '-ing' or '-ed' words.

With older children

- Read together every night – this can mean sharing a story book, looking facts up in information books, or sharing a time for silent reading.
- Help your child understand how to use reference books, dictionaries and encyclopaedias.
- Let your child buy comics or magazines – these are as important a part of the reading experience as classic fiction or detailed information books.
- Let your child see you reading – not just books, but newspapers, magazines and reference books (including things like telephone books).

WWW
Primary resources **www.primaryresources.co.uk**

This is a site aimed primary school teachers, run by practising teachers. As parents don't let it put you off. There are plenty of resources that would be useful at home.

ENGLISH

Writing

Help your child understand that writing is both useful and enjoyable by letting him see you write yourself. You don't need to be a Booker-Prize-winning author, you just need to write lists (for example, shopping lists), letters, birthday cards and so on.

You can help your child:

- plan their work;
- decide if a piece of writing could be improved;
- proof-read work (that is, check for spelling and grammatical mistakes).

But remember to let the children work things out for themselves; it's quite possible to kill a child's interest in writing by insisting on 'perfection' too early on.

Stories

You can use stories to encourage your children to read and write in many ways:

- Tell your children stories, and let them tell you stories too. Later, you can write them down – your child might like to draw pictures to go with them. Later still, your child can do the writing herself, or perhaps make up a new ending for an old story.
- Make up the beginning of a story, but stop at a cliffhanger. Let your child work out what happens next.
- Tell a story in pictures without any words at all.
- Find an interesting picture (for example, in a magazine) and tell a story to go with it.

www Alice's Adventures in Wonderland
www.typographica.com/alice

This is the complete online version of the classic story by Lewis Carroll. Beautifully illustrated, it is part of the Gutenberg Project, whose aim is to publish online books from authors who are now out of copyright.

Alice's Adventures
in Wonderland

by Lewis Carroll

typographica home   about this site

Poems

With young children, poetry is as much about playing with words for the fun of it as it is about expressing an emotion or describing a scene or piece of action.

- Read poetry aloud to your child.
- Don't forget that nursery rhymes are just poems for the very young!
- Play with words – with rhythm, rhyme and first sounds.
- Find words that sound like the action they describe (for example, miaow, screech, thump) and make poems using them.
- Make up nonsense words – can you make a poem just using them? If you can, can your child explain what he thinks is going on in it?
- Later on, introduce your child to different kinds of poems. Can he write a limerick? What about a haiku?

Aesop's Fables www.pacificnet.net/~johnr/aesop/

Most will be familiar with Aesop and his fables. This site includes over 655 fables, clearly indexed in a table with their corresponding moral. Many of the fables have been recorded in RealAudio with appropriate images. The site is great when discussing key issues with your children. For example, appearances are deceptive, leads to the fable 'The Wolf in Sheep's Clothing'. Also included are 127 fairy tales by Hans Christian Andersen with 209 'Grimms' fairy tales coming soon.

Factual writing

A grasp of factual writing will be useful across the curriculum as your child gets older. Many of the skills of factual writing also come under the general heading of 'study skills'.

- Let your child see you use writing in every day situations – such as writing lists, making notes, writing letters, even sending e-mail if you have a computer. Encourage your child to do the same (even if she can't yet write – 'pretend writing' is an important pre-writing activity).
- Help your child use writing in her everyday activities – such as making shopping lists, sending notes to friends, or taking messages when he answers the phone.
- When your child looks something up in an information book, help her to make notes. Help her to understand the difference between this kind of writing, which is purely for her own use, and the kind of writing which other people are going to see (for instance, in note-taking you don't always write in complete sentences).
- Help your child make written plans for stories and essays – help him to decide whether there is a proper beginning, middle and end, for example.

Project HappyChild **www.happychild.org.uk**

This delightfully named site is a massive project to link children all across the world. Of interest to parents looking for resources to help at home, the site contains hundreds of printable resources, including maths worksheets. Although a UK-based site, there are also links to other resources in French, German, Italian, Portuguese, Spanish and even Norwegian. On a similar international theme, HappyChild has links to over 100,000 schools worldwide. Finally, there is also a huge 'Syndromes Links' index where parents and teachers can locate help for children suffering from dyslexia, asthma, eczema and more serious conditions.

Phonics

Phonics are one of the cornerstones of the government's literacy initiative. At its most basic, teaching reading by phonics means concentrating on the sounds that the letters make, and building these up into words. This sounds very commonsensical, but there are a couple of problems. First, English isn't a phonically regular language, as a quick look at this list of words will show:

> Through
> Though
> Thought
> Cough
> Chough

This means that children also need to learn that they can't always depend on 'sounding the word out' as a strategy. Sometimes, they simply need to know what a word is – the 'look and say' method.

Second, a purely phonics-based approach makes it possible to read a word aloud without ever understanding what it means. 'Fenseted, traker, pablot, trachotting…' these are all nonsense words I just made up, but because they are phonically regular, it would be easy to read them aloud. A child – or even a teacher – could easily be fooled into thinking they were doing better than they really were because of this.

On the other hand, teaching children to read use only 'look and say' would be terribly limiting – partly because they would have to learn so many words off by heart, and partly because they wouldn't have any strategies to use when they came across new ones.

In reality, most teachers use a mixture of methods which they vary as they see fit. It's most likely that they will continue to do so – no matter what the government guidelines say.

MATHEMATICS

Helping your child with mathematics need not just be about getting them to learn their tables or making them do endless pages of sums. As with reading and writing, it's important that your child realises that mathematics is an essential part of everyday life. You can help him understand this by letting him see you use counting, adding up and so on (for instance, checking your change in the shop).

www

MathSphere **www.mathsphere.co.uk**

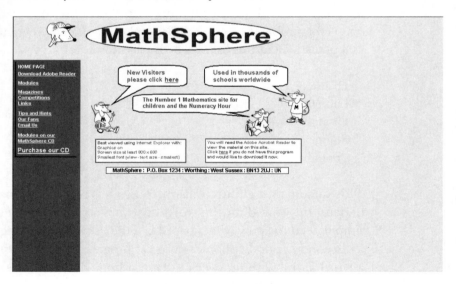

The site provides over 100 mathematics worksheets, tests, magazines, competitions, a mathematics dictionary and puzzles to print out free of charge. These are samples from a collection of 1500 similar items that are available on a CD that can be purchased from the site. Worksheets are based on the numeracy strategy introduced into UK schools in September 1999 and are therefore in line with the latest thinking in children's mathematics.

Here are some ideas for activities you can do with your child.

Number

- Teach counting games and songs like 'There Were Ten in the Bed' and 'Ten Green Bottles'.
- Play boardgames such as ludo and snakes and ladders, where you have to count as you go round the board.
- Sort and match objects – pairs of shoes; knives, forks and spoons; cups and saucers.
- Count money – how many pennies, 5p pieces etc.? Later, you can get your child to work out how much change to expect, or how much several items of shopping will cost.
- Work out how much shopping you need – how many cans of dog food you need to last a week, how many more cartons of fruit juice you must buy so she can have one a day in her lunchbox.

 ## Math Goodies **www.mathgoodies.com**

Math Goodies is a free educational website featuring interactive mathematics lessons, homework help, worksheets, puzzles and message boards. There are over 400 pages of free mathematical activities and resources for teachers, students and parents.

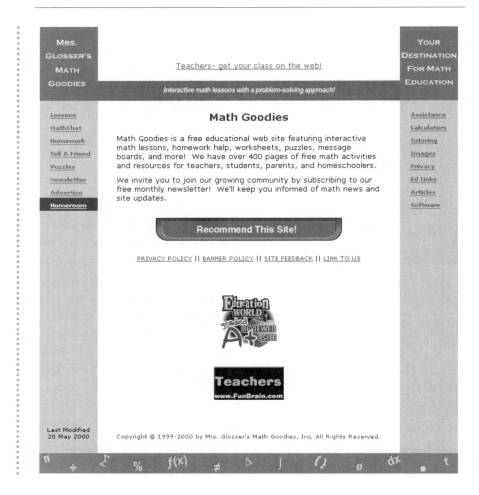

Measures

- Talk about longer and shorter, heavier and lighter.
- Play with water and sand, pouring from one container to another. Introduce words like full and empty. Discuss whether different shapes of container hold more or less, or the same amount.
- Play with weights, including weighing ingredients for cooking. Again, use appropriate language.
- Learn to tell the time, starting with the hours and moving on to half and quarter hours.

Shape and space

- Talk about the shapes you can see around you, such as triangles, rectangles, squares, circles. What makes one different from another?
- Stack boxes and cans from the store cupboard. Can your child make them fit together without any space between? How many ways can they be stacked?
- Make repeating patterns on paper. If you have three different shapes, how many different patterns can you make? What about with four? Or five? Can you make a pattern without leaving any space between the shapes (no overlapping!)? Are there any shapes you can't do this with?
- Similarly, build shapes out of Lego.
- Explore symmetry by folding paper in halves and quarters and cutting out patterns, or by drawing a pattern on one side of the paper and copying it on the other. Or make 'butterflies' by splashing paint on a piece of paper and folding it in half.

The language of mathematics

It's easy to think of mathematics as something to be understood – a set of concepts, such as what you're really doing when you 'carry one' in an addition sum; and even easier to see it as a skill to be used – how to add up and perform other arithmetical operations, how to work out area and volume, and how to use mathematical instruments such as rulers, protractors and weighing scales.

But neither of these are any use to your child if he doesn't know how to bring mathematics into his everyday life, and how to understand the different ways we have of talking about mathematics and discussing mathematical problems. This is an area where you can really make a difference – all you have to do is find different ways of talking about what you're doing when you carry out simple every day activities such as shopping, cooking and watching television.

 The most important thing is to find different ways of expressing ideas, rather than letting your child get the idea that there is only one right way. It's impossible to list all the different variations you could use, but here you'll find some examples in each area of mathematics. You'll notice that not all of these are totally grammatical – that's because people don't necessarily talk in 'proper English'!

Addition

- Add three and five.
- What do you get if you add three and five?
- What do three and five come to?
- If I have three, and you give me five more, how many do I have altogether?
- Three and five is … ?
- Three plus five make?
- How many do three and five make?

Subtraction

- What is nine minus six?
- What do you get if you take six from nine?
- If I have nine, and I give you six, how many do I have left?
- How many are left over if you take six away from nine?
- Six from nine is … ?
- Subtract six from nine.
- What is nine subtract six?

Multiplication

- What are seven eights?
- What are eight lots of seven?
- What do you get if you multiply eight by seven?
- What is eight by seven?
- If there are eight children, and they each have seven apples, how many apples is that altogether?
- Times eight by seven.

Division

- Divide 14 by 7.
- What is 14 divided by 7?
- Share 14 oranges between 7 people.
- Put 14 into 7 groups.
- If I share 14 oranges between 7 people, how many oranges does each person get?

Length

- How long is this?
- What is the length of this?
- Is this longer than that?
- Is this shorter than that?
- Is this long enough?
- Which of these is the longest?
- Which of these is the shortest?
- How much longer than that is this?
- How much shorter than this is that?
- How high is that?
- What height is that?

Weight

- How much does this weigh?
- Is this heavy?
- Is this light?
- Is this lighter than that?
- Which of these is the heaviest?
- What weight is this?
- Does this weigh enough?
- Is this heavier than that?

Area

- This room is 15 metres wide by 20 long.
- Is the carpet big enough to cover the floor?
- What size is that piece of paper?

- This is 10 centimetres square.
- This is 10 square centimetres.
- What is the area of that wall?
- Which of these is bigger – the envelope or the stamp?

Volume

- How much shampoo is there?
- There's half a litre of milk left.
- Is the bottle big enough to take all the orange juice?
- Will the orange juice fit in the bottle?
- Is there more orange juice or milk left?

The Clock

- What time is it?
- Could you tell me the time, please?
- It's exactly 12 noon.
- It's three fifteen.
- The time is quarter past three.
- It's quarter to four.
- It's four pm.

Timetables

- Am I early?
- The bus is late!
- What time is Rugrats on?
- Three minutes to go!
- We've got half-an-hour to get there …
- The next bus will be here in 15 minutes.
- Who got here first?
- Ahmed got here before Clare.
- Zainab got here after Roy.

The CD contains a selection of Numeracy-based games and worksheets; further examples can be found at **www.parents.org.uk**

Mathematical Investigations

Mathematics isn't just about facts (such as the times tables), it's also about problem solving – first working out what the problem is, then trying out different ways of solving it, and then deciding which is best and why. Mathematical investigations may look a bit haphazard, but done properly they help children think more clearly and logically, and record and communicate what they have found out.

Try this investigation with your child:

- Take the lace out of a trainer.
- Ask your child to put it back in. How many ways can she find to do it?
- How can she be sure she's found all the different ways?
- Can she find a way of recording what she's done, so as to help her keep track and show other people what she has done?

Some teachers would suggest to the children that they record what they are doing right at the beginning of the exercise. Others would let the children work out that it's a good idea for themselves. Unsurprisingly, children who have done a lot of investigations tend to think of recording it immediately!

Bases

In mathematics, this is the number of single digits allowed by a system of counting. Although this is a simple concept, it forms the basis of all of the rest of arithmetic, so it's important children understand it thoroughly.

In most everyday mathematics, we use base 10. This means we use the digits 0, 1, 2, 3, 4, 5, 6, 7, 8, 9 – almost certainly because we have 10 fingers and thumbs. However, certain other bases are also used (though some of them are being phased out). For example:

- computers use base 2 – binary – in which the only digits are 0 and 1;
- in telling the time, we use base 60 (for the number of seconds in the minute and the number of minutes in the hour) and either base 12 or 24 (for the number of hours in a day by the am/pm or the 24-hour system);
- in measuring angle, we use base 60 and base 360 to express degrees of arc;
- in measuring using imperial weights, we use base 16 and 14 (ounces to pounds and pounds to stones);
- the old fogies among us are used to using base 12 and even base 3 for measuring inches to the foot and feet to the yard.

In theory, for bases above 10 it's necessary to invent extra symbols for the single digits over 9. Hexadecimal – base 16, used in computer programming – does this by using the letters of the alphabet to represent them. In practice, though, most everyday bases larger than 10 don't bother with special symbols.

It can help children a lot to have these other bases pointed out to them. In fact, practising counting anything that comes in sets of a given number will help your child grasp the concept. If you want a simple example, try showing them boxes of eggs (either in half-dozen or dozen sizes – base 6 and base 12); or you could count gloves, shoes, or socks in base 2 – 'I've got five socks, so that that's two pairs and one left over'.

Arithmetic

Basic arithmetic is easy once you understand what you are doing in the process. This may sound like a statement of the obvious, but if you have ever tried to explain a mathematical operation to a child who 'can't see' the process, you will understand what they mean.

Addition

Addition is essentially joining two or more groups of objects/numbers, to make a larger single group. Children will understand this very quickly. The challenging part is finding a way of recording, or writing down what they are doing.

Numerals, digits and numbers

The first thing children need to recognise are the 10 numerals/digits – 0, 1, 2, 3, 4, 5, 6, 7, 8, 9 – and then to know that all numbers in our counting system are represented by the way we write down combinations of the numerals. The next stage is knowing that the position of a numeral to a number determines what its actual value is. This is called 'place value'. For example, 7 is not worth the same as 170 or 7700.

A useful way of helping children with understanding numerals is to compare numbers with words and numerals/digits with letters. In the same way we join letters together to make words, we join numerals/digits together to make numbers. Some numbers are only one numeral/digit long, others are much longer.

Amongst the first things children learn in school, is to memorise the number bonds to make 5 and then 10. In the early stages of mathematical computation, the more reference that is made to these bonds, the faster the children will progress.

Example techniques

The important action is to break the sum down into more manageable mini sums :

$7 + 9 = ?$ ... don't do it, change the sum:
$7 + 10 = 17$
Next, take away the extra 1 added to the 9:
$17 - 1 = 16$

Parents Online (**www.parents.org.uk**) has plenty of other examples, including techniques for subtraction, division and multiplication.

Commutativity in mathematics

This isn't a word your child is likely to hear during mathematics lessons, but it's still an important concept. It simply means that you can carry out mathematical operations (such as adding, subtracting, multiplying and dividing) either way round and still get the same result.

Adding and multiplying are commutative:

> The answer to the sum
> $3 + 8$ is 11. So is the answer to the sum $8 + 3$.
> Similarly, $8 \times 3 = 24$ – and so does 3×8.
> However, if you consider the sum $15 - 8 = 7$
> it is clear that you get a different answer than you would if you took fifteen from eight $(8 - 15)$.

Division works the same way: six divided by three gives a different answer than three divided by six.

Although this probably seems perfectly straightforward, quite a number of children find it difficult to grasp, and a lack of understanding can lead to hard-to-spot errors in their number work.

Tessellation

Tessellation is a way of making patterns out of smaller shapes. The word comes from *tesserae* – the small tiles used to make mosaics. When teachers talk about tessellation, they tend to mean making patterns that can be repeated indefinitely using regular shapes, without overlapping them or leaving spaces between them. Studying tessellation helps children learn about the properties of two-dimensional shapes.

Sometimes teachers ask children to make a pattern using only one shape; sometimes the activity will involve using more than one shape; and sometimes the children will be asked to discover which shapes will tessellate and which will not. The activity may be left purely as a mathematical exercise, or it can be extended into other areas – for example, by exploring different ways of emphasising the repeating patterns by using colour, or using tessellated patterns as surface decoration in a design project.

 You can try this for yourself by printing off a range of shapes (squares, oblongs, triangles of different types, pentagons, hexagons, etc.), cutting them out and using them as templates.

Symmetry

Symmetry is a property of two-dimensional objects. It means that the object is shaped the same on both sides – you could fold it in half along an imaginary axis, and the sides would match. This is called lateral symmetry. There is another type of symmetry – rotational symmetry. The difference is, instead of folding the object, you spin it around a point.

In school, children are often asked to explore symmetry in two ways – by deciding which objects are symmetrical, and by creating symmetrical objects themselves. They usually have to identify and mark the axis (or point) of symmetry.

Here are some examples of laterally symmetrical objects:

- humans (at least externally – our internal organs aren't arranged symmetrically);
- a domino;
- a pair of scissors;
- a starfish (if you draw the axis so that it divides one arm);
- the letters B C D E H I K M O T U V W X;
- a butterfly.

And rotationally symmetrical objects:

- A starfish;
- a butcher's hook;
- the letters S N X Z.

You'll notice that quite a few objects have more than one axis of symmetry, and that some have both lateral and rotational symmetry.

Symmetry investigations

- Find some objects and ask/decide if they are symmetrical or not. Find the axis or point of symmetry. Prove you're right – mark the axis and fold the object, or the point and spin it. If the object isn't something you can fold, draw round it on a piece of paper and cut it out first.

- Splash paint (the sort that comes in squeezy bottles is great for this) on a piece of paper. Fold the paper in half and open it out to find a symmetrical 'butterfly'. Can you see other patterns there?

Polyominoes

You'll need some squared paper – 1cm squares are best. If you cut out one of the squares, there's only one way to do it. If you cut out two squares (a domino), there is also only one way to do it. But if you cut out three square's there are two ways – you can make a strip of three; or an 'L' shape.

Ask your child to discover how many ways there are to cut out four squares, and then five and six – always remembering that the squares must be joined along an edge, not just at a corner. Now – which of these shapes are symmetrical? How many have more than one axis of symmetry? Which have lateral symmetry and which rotational symmetry? How many have both? Neither?

Could you use the polyominoes to make a poster to teach someone about symmetry?

SCIENCE

At its simplest, science is a way to understand the world by observing, recording and making theories and testing them. This may sound daunting, but it can also be great fun. Don't forget that at the primary-school level a lot of science comes down to commonsense and logic.

You can help your child by:

- Exploring the world using the senses – taste, smell, hearing, sight and touch.
- Naming things – such as the parts of the human body and plants and animals.
- Sorting things into categories and discussing why they belong there.

- Observing how things change – for example, the seasons; the way young animals grow; or (if you can stand it!) the way food 'goes off'.
- Keeping a pet – what does it need to stay healthy? Are these the same things that your child needs?
- Growing plants – what do they need to do well?
- Exploring the way every-day materials can be changed – what happens when water is heated or frozen? What about when you put sugar in tea? Can you get the sugar back out of the tea? What's the difference between doing that and mixing sand and water?
- Watching what happens when you drop a ball. What about rolling it down a slope? What can you do to make it go faster or slower (for example, change the slant of the slope, push the ball harder, make the surface rougher to increase friction)?
- Talking about electricity and why we need it. Discuss the fact that it is also dangerous.
- Visiting science museums, open farms, planetariums and so on.

Natural History Museum **www.nhm.ac.uk**

The official site for the Natural History Museum contains all the usual visitors' information that you would expect. There is a growing number of online exhibits allowing you to enjoy the museum's treasures from the comfort of your own home 365 days a year. We particularly liked 'AntCast' a webcam (relaying pictures) on the crazy world of ants.

Science experiments

To non-scientists, science may sound a bit daunting, but it's really just a way of finding out about the world in a consistent and organised fashion. However complicated it gets, science can be broken down into a few steps:

- observing and recording
- making a theory
- testing the theory and recording the results
- adjusting the theory to fit the results you got.

Most of this is pretty straightforward, but there are a few points about testing that children sometimes have difficulty getting to grips with. These are all to do with making sure you get a valid result. These points also apply to testing materials and constructions in Design Technology.

Bizzare stuff **freeweb.pdq.net/headstrong**

This site is a museum of classic home-science experiments, mainly from the 1930s–1960s. Don't let the dates put you off – these experiments using household items truly demonstrate many of the scientific principles that are so important to modern life. As examples, you can make electric motors, cameras and even radios.

- **Know what you're testing** – for example, you might make paper aeroplanes and then test them to see which flies best. But what does best mean? Is it the one that flies furthest, even if it spirals out of control? Is it the one that flies most smoothly? Or the one that stays level for longest?

- **Compare like with like** – for example, you can't measure one distance in metres and another in yards.
- **Tests have to be fair** – if you're trying to work out which of two things works best, you have to test them in the same way. For example, if you're trying to decide which of two paper aeroplanes flies furthest, you need to start them off at the same height and in the same conditions (inside or outside; windy or not windy).
- **Only change one variable at a time** – if you change more than one variable, you won't be able to tell which one caused the difference in your new results. For example, if you decide to improve your paper aeroplane by using lighter, stiffer paper, and a design with wider wings and a longer tail, you may very well succeed – but you won't know which of the four things you changed made the difference.

Thursday's Classroom **www.thursdaysclassroom.com**

The aim of Thursday's Classroom is to provide a lasting connection between NASA's latest research and the classroom environment. The site contains lesson plans, resources and stories with reference to space. There is also access to NASA's rich library of images and video clips.

Ecology

Ecology is the part of science that investigates the relationships between living creatures and how they depend on each other. It's impossible to understand environmental issues without some under-standing of ecology.

The particular role a creature or plant takes in its region is called an 'ecological niche'. Various factors affect whether the organism can keep its place. These include the availability of food and suitable breeding sites, and whether or not the creature can evade predators. Things do tend to balance out. For example, if there are too many predators, the animals or plants they feed on will die out; but this will result in their being fewer predators over time, which will – other things being equal – allow the number of food, animals or plants to rise again.

One of the most important relationships is, basically, 'who eats who'. This is called a food chain. An example of a food chain might be: grass > antelope > lion (with decomposers processing the dead bodies of both the antelope and the lion, and dead plant material). However, in the real world things aren't quite so simple, and what actually happens is that there are many food chains that interlink. These make a food web.

Different organisms play different roles in the ecology – and sometimes more than one. Green plants get their energy from the sun. They are eaten by herbivores – grazing and browsing animals – which are eaten by carnivores – meat eaters. Carnivores are at the top of the food chain. Nothing eats them, unless they die of natural causes or are killed by humans. Decomposers live on the dead remains of plants and animals, breaking them down; they use some of the nutrients as food, but the rest returns to the environment. The most numerous of the decomposers are fungi and bacteria, but others include earthworms and beetles.

As you can see, harming one animal or plant in a food chain can have a profound effect on all the others.

Factors that can affect the organisms in a particular area include:

• food supply
• pollution
• loss of breeding habitat
• water supply
• hunting
• presence of human artefacts such as roads.

Classifying things

One of the basic skills children need to learn is that of classifying things – sorting them into groups (called 'sets' in mathematics) according to their properties. You can break this down into several parts:

• classifying things according to existing criteria;
• classifying things according to several criteria at once;

- learning that the same object can belong in several different sets, and how to choose the most appropriate classification;
- working out a classification system of their own;
- deciding what to do when there is no clear classification system to use.

Here are some examples of each of these, with mini-activities you can do to explore some of them:

Classifying things according to existing criteria

Get a jumble of objects and sort them according to these classifications:

- living (animals, plants, people);
- dead; non-living (bricks, plastic, metal);
- things that come in pairs (hands, feet, socks, shoes, gloves, chopsticks);
- white things – snow, milk, writing paper.

What other criteria could you use? Don't forget that you might need a set that consists of 'things that don't fit anywhere' (this is a trickier concept for some children to grasp than you might expect).

Classifying things according to several criteria at once

Choose some different objects. This time, sort them into sets that have more than one thing in common:

- things to wear that are green;
- things to drink that are clear (lemonade, water);
- things that are alive that you might find in your home (people, pets ... pests?).

Learning that the same object can belong in several different sets

You will probably need to choose the objects, and the sets, for this investigation with a bit more care. For example, you might have a tin can, a dead fish, a pile of sand, a shell, a piece of plastic, a pair of welling-tons, and an umbrella. If the sets available are:

- rubbish
- things I might find on the beach
- things I use when it rains,

then it's obvious that some of the items will fit easily into each of the categories. But the dead fish, the tin can and the plastic might all be found on the beach and yet also be classed as rubbish.

Working out a classification system of their own

This time, instead of telling the child the category and asking which objects fit it, do the reverse – talk about the object and what it's like, and then decide on a category. You might find that you have seven objects and seven categories, in which case you will need to decide how to group them together better – or perhaps decide that there is no way of grouping them that isn't com-pletely forced ('things that are black, green or white and that you find in the kitchen or garden ...').

Deciding what to do when there is no clear classification system to use

Sometimes categories are too subjective. For exam-ple, a group of 'long things' sounds fine until you discover that one person thinks something is long, but someone else is convinced that it is short. You'll probably need to choose some objects to discuss to make this clear. What does your child think you could do about it? One suggestion might be to change the category a bit – so 'long things' become 'things that are longer than my arm', for example.

INFORMATION AND COMMUNICATION TECHNOLOGY (ICT)

Not everyone has a computer at home (and you shouldn't feel pressured into buying one if you can't afford it), so there probably won't be homework in ICT. However, ICT is important now, and will only get more important in the future, so it is a good idea to help your child understand it if you can.

- Introduce the idea that the computer can be useful as well as fun.
- Show your child how to use the word processor to write letters and stories. Don't forget to show him how to save, retrieve and print out his work. Later, you can introduce the idea of revising work and proof-reading.
- Use a drawing package to make pictures and borders to decorate work.
- Use a simple database to organise information (for example, your child's video collection), and a spreadsheet package to present it in graphs and charts.
- Don't forget that your child can use the computer to help with homework both by writing stories and reports on it, and to find information in educational CD-ROMs and on the internet.
- Consider getting educational software – don't forget that ICT is used across the curriculum, so programs or multimedia that support subjects like history, geography, science and design technology can be a good investment.
- If you have an internet connection, use it to find information using search engines (but take care if your child uses the internet alone – not everything that is available is suitable for children. You might want to consider using a 'blocker' programme to limit your child's access to certain websites or newsgroups).
- Perhaps your child could get an e-mail pen-pal (best arranged by your child's school 'twinning' with one in another country); but take care that anyone your child e-mails is genuine, especially if they find them from a newsgroup.

- Don't dismiss games – they can help to develop your child's decision-making and problem-solving abilities, as well as help his reflexes!
- Finally, don't let your child spend all his time on the computer. Computers may be fun and useful, but they're no substitute for flesh-and-blood friendships or exploring the real world.

HISTORY

History is a fascinating subject, but it can be a bit remote for young children. Help your child understand history by starting with the changes that have taken place in her own lifetime, and work outwards from there.

- Explore and discuss how things change over time (for instance, the way your child's body grows; changes in the local area such as shops closing down and new ones taking their place; additions to the family such as new brothers, sisters or cousins – or even pets!). Use words like 'before' and 'after', and 'earlier' and 'later'.
- Make a timeline. This could include events in the child's life such as when she was born, when she started school and when she got pets or special toys. Later, you can include other events – other people's birthdates, family events such as births and marriages, holidays, and so on; you can also include events from outside the family, such as sporting occasions. With older children, you can extend the timeline back, and include world events such as changes of government, the dates of wars and so on.
- Encourage your child to keep a diary, including dates of important events during the year such as family birthdays and holidays.
- Use books, videos and pictures to explore the differences between past times and life today, including the way people lived, dressed and ate.
- Point out buildings in different styles of architecture and encourage your child to think about when they might have been erected.

- Investigate famous people from the past, such as Guy Fawkes, using books and CD-ROMs.
- Visit museums and discuss what you see there – and take advantage if they run workshops or 'hands-on' days.
- Encourage your child to talk to older members of the family about the differences between when they were young and life nowadays.

Public Record Office www.pro.gov.uk/education/primary.htm

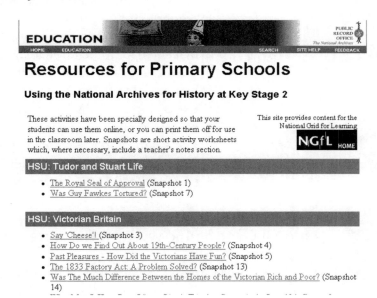

This is the educational section of the Public Record Office, with activities and worksheets to download relating to key historical events.

GEOGRAPHY

As with history, the best way to introduce geography is by starting with what your child already knows – his home and the area around it.

- Explore the local area with your child and talk about what you find (for example, roads, shops, parks, fields, woods).
- Play games that help your child to understand directions (such as a variation on 'hunt the thimble' where he is given instructions such as 'left', 'right', 'up' and 'down'; later on, you can introduce the use of a compass and directions including 'east', 'west' and so on).
- Help your child to make a plan of his bedroom, showing where all the furniture is (if you cut pictures of the furniture out of card, he can move it around – though this might lead him to want to move the real furniture too!); later on, you can make a map of the local area, and perhaps introduce the idea of scale. Use the map to work out new routes to the shops and to school.
- Use pictures, videos, books and CD-ROMs to find out about other places in the world. Find them on maps and globes (see **www.parents.org.uk** for latest suggestions). Talk about how and why life there might be different from the way it is here.

National Geographic **www.nationalgeographic.com**

This site of the famous magazine has plenty to offer families. Here you will find much of their lavish photography, maps and stories from around the world. For children, the special kids section contains plenty of scientific facts presented in an easy to use manner.

DESIGN AND TECHNOLOGY

You can help your child with design and technology by encouraging her to design and make things at home. This needn't involve a lot of expense or complicated equipment. Do remember to teach your child to work safely, and with adult supervision where necessary. Also remember that design and technology teaches the skills of planning, evaluation and improving ones work, as well as allowing children to explore the use of materials, processes and techniques.

- Talk about objects and equipment you use around the house every day. Discuss how well they do their jobs, whether they look good and are reliable, and whether they make you want to use them. How could they be improved?
- When your child's found a board game she enjoys (or perhaps one she doesn't!), suggest she use the pieces to make up one of her own. She'll need to test the rules, and perhaps eventually write them down. She could also make her own board and playing pieces.

All Mixed Up www.allmixedup.com

Game fads come and go, but it is always that old favorite such as hangman that we return to. All Mixed Up includes some of the classic games: clunk, hangman, Tic Tac Toe, Connect 4, Othello, Slider Ataxx, Solo, Kona, light, Merlin, paint, Solitaire, Yahtzee. These are implemented online and challenge you to play the computer.

- Let your child cook, making sure he follows a recipe and measures and weighs the ingredients. Again, he could explore ways to change the recipe. Hold a family tasting session to decide what worked best and why.

- Use construction toys like Lego and Meccano. Encourage your child to plan ahead, as well as just making things up as he goes along.
- Teach your child to sew and knit. This could include embroidery and patchwork as well as making items like pencil cases. Consider buying a child's sewing machine. Older children can start to work from patterns. Remember to help your child to plan his work and to decide how well it came out afterwards.
- Make models from card, boxes, balsa wood and other simple materials. Explore the use of glue, tape and pins to fix things together (older children can use tacks and a light hammer with adult supervision). Find ways of making moveable joints (for example, by making fabric hinges). You could copy famous buildings or vehicles (such as Big Ben or the Lunar Landing Module), or invent your own.
- Explore flight by making paper aeroplanes, kites and gliders.
- Explore floating and buoyancy by making boats and submarines.
- Use batteries, torch bulbs and switches to explore electricity (you could use a kit to start you off if this seems daunting). Remember to emphasise the difference between safe exploration and using mains power.

ART

As with music, the point of teaching art is both to help your child appreciate it, and to help them create their own art.

- Provide your child with art materials such as paper, paints, crayons, card, glue and modelling clay (you can get clay that will harden in an ordinary oven).
- Draw, paint and model with your child. Remember, it's

not so much the finished product that matters as the experience of making it (in other words, don't worry if you think you can't draw – just enjoy having a go!).

- Especially with younger children, explore ways of expressing emotion through art as well as making realistic drawings and paintings.
- Draw from real life – look closely at an object or scene, and try to get down on paper exactly what you see. Talk about the kinds of patterns and textures you can see, and how you could reproduce them on paper.
- Help your child to explore colour mixing and matching with paints and soluble pencils. What colours do you have to mix to make a particular colour? Are there any colours you can't make by mixing? Look at DIY paint charts and colour wheels, and see if you can work out why they are arranged the way they are.
- Look at colours and patterns in nature and in the built environment. Do patterns repeat? Are they always identical, or are there small variations?
- Let your child choose posters, pictures and photographs to go in her bedroom. Talk about why she likes certain ones better than others. Discuss why you chose the pictures on your walls as well.
- Talk about artists, the kinds of work they produce and what they were trying to achieve (it's probably easiest to pick artists with a distinctive style, such as Lowry, Turner, Monet and Van Gogh).
- Visit art galleries, museums and country houses. Discuss what you see there. In particular, talk about the way people lived and the kinds of things they liked to have around them.
- Visit craft shows, and let your child see the kinds of things people make today. If there are demonstrations, so much the better. If your child is interested, see if she can talk to the craftspeople about what they do and why.

Cartoon Corner www.cartooncorner.com

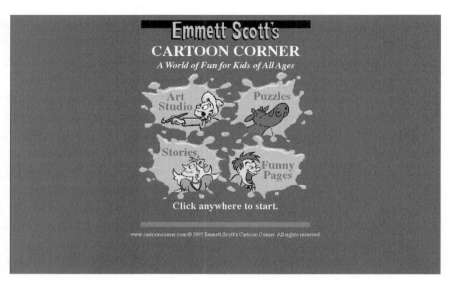

A site devoted to cartoons for all ages; here you can learn how to draw cartoons, including caricatures and spot drawings. There are also puzzles and pictures to download to print and colour.

Mixing colours

When we talk about mixing colour, we generally mean mixing pigment. This is called subtractive mixing.

When white light hits a coloured surface, most of it is absorbed, but some of it is reflected – and that's the part we can see. Thus, a green object reflects green light but absorbs all the other wavelengths.

When we mix pigments, more light is absorbed. If you could mix paint perfectly, it would be black – all the light would be absorbed. This is why mixing pigment is called subtractive mixing.

There are some colours of pigment you can make by mixing other colours, and some you can't. Those you can't make are red, blue and yellow. They are called primary colours. The colours you get when you mix any two of them are called secondary colours. Here's what you get:

- red and yellow = orange
- yellow and blue = green
- blue and red = purple (or sometimes brown, depending on the primary shades you use).

Obviously, the exact shade you get depends on the colours you start with and the proportions you mix them in.

It is possible to make a colour wheel, in which the colours are graduated into each other. This works best if you have a true primary red, blue and yellow to work with – ask for advice in an art shop, if you aren't certain what to use.

Start by cutting out a circle of card. Divide it into three with pencil lines. Paint over each line with a strip of red, blue, or yellow. Now, starting with the red, carefully blend in a little yellow. Paint in a stripe of that colour. Then mix more and more yellow with the red, painting a stripe of each colour on your wheel, until you get a pure yellow. Now start mixing in blue – again, paint stripes of the colours you make, until you arrive at pure blue. Then work from blue to red.

If you look at your colour wheel, you'll see that the contrast between colours directly opposite each other is particularly strong. These are called complementary colours – thus, red is complementary to green, and so on.

There is one other property of colour you can explore, and that is saturation. This means how much white the colour is mixed with. You can explore this by making a colour bar that graduates from any strong colour (not necessarily a primary colour) to white, and back again.

MUSIC

There are two ways you can help your child with music – by helping her become a confident singer or performer, and by helping him enjoy and appreciate listening to music.

- Let your child see that you enjoy music – have it playing in the background as you work, but also just sit down and listen to it.
- Play different kinds of music at home – pop, folk, classical, hymns, carols and other religious music. Include music from different cultures and times.
- Sing with your child – anything from nursery rhymes to traditional songs to the latest pop songs.

- If you can play an instrument, play to your child. Let him see you practising, too.
- Play rhythm games – for example, tap a rhythm and let your child tap it back to you, or continue the rhythm.
- Help your child to make up songs and tunes, and work out words to go with them.
- Talk about music – pick out the instruments in a piece of music; talk to your child about how a particular song makes him feel; discuss what kinds of music you like and share information about them.
- Go to concerts with your child.
- Give your child the opportunity to learn an instrument (this may be available at school), and encourage her to practise regularly.

KidsMusic www.kidsmusic.co.uk

This is the site of the publishers of all those music and sing-along cassettes that support many of the popular children's TV series such as *Postman Pat*, *Sesame Street*, *Teletubbies*, *Mopatop*, *Mr Men* and *Little Miss*,

Barney, and *Paddington Bear*. Not only can you order the cassettes online but you can also download sample tracks to your computer.

PHYSICAL EDUCATION

Obviously, it's unlikely that your child will be set PE homework. However, you can help your child to become physically active, skilled and confident.

- Take your child out walking. You can walk to school and in familiar places like the park, but you could also go further afield.
- Play throwing and catching games like netball, and bat-and-ball games like short tennis, rounders and cricket.
- Encourage your child to dance when you have music on.
- Don't forget games that help to develop fine muscle control, such as pick-a-sticks, fives and playing with a yo-yo.
- Consider letting your child take gymnastics, dance or martial arts training (but be sure the instructors are fully qualified, that their equipment is well maintained and that they enforce proper safety rules).
- Make sure your child learns to swim (either take her yourself or let her have lessons).
- Encourage your child to join a group, such as Brownies or Cubs, where they play team games.
- If you do a sport yourself, encourage your child to join in where appropriate.
- If you follow a sport, encourage your child to take an interest – not only by watching it on television, but also by going to matches.

Football365 www.football365.com

For football fans this is an excellent starting point, with all the latest news from the game and clubs in the top two divisions. There are also games, puzzles and trivia to keep you amused. Most clubs will also have their own sites and details of how to get involved.

RELIGIOUS EDUCATION

If you have strong beliefs yourself, you will undoubtedly want to teach your child about your faith and help him to take a part in the religious life of your community. However, even if you don't consider yourself to be religious, you may still want to help your child to understand the beliefs other people hold.

- Help your child to investigate the meaning of the big national celebrations – Christmas and Easter. What significance do they hold for Christians? Do other faiths have similar festivals? Why is Christmas in mid-winter? Why are eggs an Easter symbol?
- Explore the feasts of religions other than Christianity, such as Hannukah, Eid, Diwali and Ramadan. Again, look for similarities and differences between them.
- Look for churches, mosques, synagogues and other religious buildings in your local area or the nearest big town. Do they have anything in common? If they have an 'open door' policy, you can look inside. If not, you can at least examine them from outside.
- Explore the art of different religious faiths, such as Christian stained-glass windows, Orthodox Christian icons, and Islamic geometric patterns. Could your child use them as a basis for his own work?
- Explore stories from the Bible and other religious books. Can your child use them as the basis for his own stories?
- Discuss the values that religions have in common, such as honesty, caring, peace and justice. Explore why these are held in common, and how they form a good basis for living, whether or not you are religious.

Part 3

Leisure and health

● ● ● ● ● ● ● ● ● ● ● ● ● ● ● ●

- After-school activities
- Keeping pets
- Parties
- Leisure tips
- Health

CHAPTER 8

After-school activities

● ● ● ● ● ● ● ● ● ● ● ● ● ● ● ● ●

Your child's education is important – but so is what happens out of school. Children need time for unstructured play, to help them assimilate what they have learned and to develop independence and creativity. Some children also thrive on the kind of structure provided by organised group activities. But for a healthy relationship, they also need time with you – time when you are just having fun together.

In this chapter, you'll find information on organisations and groups your child can join, and things you can do as a family – whether you've got an hour, an afternoon, or a day to spare. Quite apart from the enjoyment your child may get from the activities, there are other good reasons for encouraging them to take part:

- they may meet different children – possibly from a different range of backgrounds; not only is this fun, it may also help children who are shy, or who are having difficulty at school build their confidence;
- they will have a chance to relate to adults in a slightly different way than they do either with teachers or members of their family;
- by offering a different range of possibilities, such activities offer children the chance to build different skills – this can be especially helpful for children who are having difficulty with formal schoolwork;

- as the government places more emphasis on literacy, numeracy and the requirements of the national curriculum, some schools are finding it difficult to find time for art, drama and other creative activities, and sport – out-of-school activities can pick up the slack;
- and don't forget – activities give parents a break!

So, what's available? Broadly speaking, there are four kinds of out-of-school activities:

- organised group activities such as Brownies, Cub Scouts and others;
- after-school clubs organised by the school itself, or your local authority;
- classes in drama, art, and other creative activities;
- formal and informal sports training and sessions.

ORGANISED ACTIVITIES

The best known of the organised activities are undoubtedly the Guides and the Scouts, and their junior sections the Brownies and Cubs. However, there are a couple of other options you might want to consider, especially if you'd prefer your child to be in a mixed-sex environment.

All these groups stress the importance of developing self-esteem, tolerance, understanding and self-discipline, and they all offer a wide range of creative, sporting and practical activities, plus excursions, camping trips and so on. Beyond that, there are some differences in style and emphasis, and it would probably be worthwhile talking to the leaders of your local groups, and perhaps visiting (if that is allowed) before you and your child make a decision about joining.

Guides

This organisation provides activities for girls and young women from the age of five:

- Rainbow Guides (5 years and over; or, in Ulster, from the fourth birthday)
- Brownie Guides (7 years and over)
- Guides (10 years and over)
- Senior Section (14 to 25 years).

Girls are able to join (or leave) at any point – it isn't necessary to start at the bottom and work all the way through. Membership is open to girls of all backgrounds and faiths.

There's quite a lot of research that shows that girls do better academically in single-sex schools, perhaps because it's easier for them to get attention and build self-esteem. The Guides might be of special benefit to quieter girls, especially if they seem a bit lost or overlooked in a mixed-sex primary school.

The Guides are a uniformed organisation, but their Trefoil Guild section offers a similar range of activities without the uniform, and, perhaps, in a less formal atmosphere.

The Guide Association **www.guides.org.uk**

General information about the Guide Association, including basic details about Rainbows, Brownies, Guides, Senior Section and adult members, including their Promise and uniform. Read about the history of the Guide Association and learn about International Guiding – including Thinking Day, WAGGGS, and the Guide Friendship Fund. There are ideas, news and activity things to try for each Section; places to go and things to see, such as the Guide Heritage Centre, World Centres, Training and Activity Centres; and links to other Guiding-related websites. You can also find Guide Association news, contact details, information on internet safety, the Guide Association's latest publications and downloadable documents.

Scouts

Like the Guides, the Scouts offer a formal, uniformed organisation and a range of activities. Unlike the Guides – and perhaps contrary to most people's expectations – the Scouts are open to both boys and girls. The emphasis is on outdoor and practical activities, but that now includes a number of exciting activities such as racing home-made vehicles. There are special sections for Air Scouts and Sea Scouts.

There are different sections for different ages:

- Beaver Scouts (6 and 7-year-olds)
- Cub Scouts (8 to $10\frac{1}{2}$-year-olds)
- Scouts ($10\frac{1}{2}$ to $15\frac{1}{2}$-year-olds).

Scouting www.scoutnet.org.uk

This is a useful site if you're interested in Scouting. The site features Baloo, which is a search engine intended to help you find Scouting-related information on the web. If you have a scouting site, you can submit the URL for indexing by Baloo. The site also links to **www.scoutbase.org.uk** which is the official website of the Scout Association. There is information on official Scouting publications, major Scouting sites, Scouting resources, games, ideas, contacts and much more. Scouting software (clipart etc. for PC and Mac) can be downloaded. You can also view scouting homepages, join newsgroups and express your opinion on Scouting issues through interactive message bases.

St John Ambulance

St John Ambulance is, of course, well known for its first aid training. There are over 57,000 St John Ambulance volunteers, and over half of them are in its junior sections:

• Badgers (6 to 10-year-olds)
• Cadets (10 to 16-year-olds).

Badgers' activities are a mixture of first aid and safety training, and outdoor pursuits, though activities can include everything from cookery to gardening. Cadets receive training in first aid, social care and communications. There are also social events and excursions.

St John Ambulance www.st-john-ambulance.org.uk

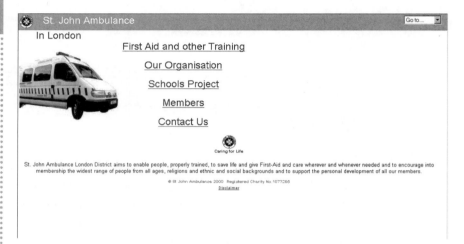

St John Ambulance is the UK's leading first aid, transport and care charity. Its mission is to provide first aid and medical support services, caring services in support of community needs and education, and training and personal development to young people. St John Ambulance teaches comprehensive first aid to individuals, groups, employees and volunteers. Every year it trains 500,000 people and treats 200,000 casualties. You can learn about the organisation's history, aims and organisation at this site. Local and national activities are described and contact information is provided. Look also at **www.london.sja.org.uk/sites.htm** for a search engine which links you to a wide variety of information.

Woodcraft Folk

The Woodcraft Folk is the children and youth's organisation of the co-operative movement. Its motto is 'Span The World With Friendship'.

Children are divided by age range:

• Elfins (6 to 9-year-olds)
• Pioneers (10 to 12-year-olds)
• Venturers (13 to 15-year-olds)
• District Fellowship (16 to 20-year-olds).

The Woodcraft Folk provide a range of activities, including crafts, drama, singing, outdoor pursuits and games. There's a strong emphasis on international understanding, which is supported by an active exchange programme. See the website **www.poptel.org.uk/ woodcraft/** for more information.

AFTER-SCHOOL CLUBS

Some schools have after-school clubs on the premises. They may be run by teachers (either volunteering or paid – often by the local council's youth service, rather than its education department), or by play workers employed by the youth service. Sometimes they welcome children from other schools. In addition to a range of fun activities such as sports, games and crafts, they sometimes incorporate a homework club, especially for older children.

In some areas, after-school clubs are held in specialist play centres. These will often offer weekend and holiday provision, too.

After-school clubs tend not to go on very late in the evening, but in addition to providing extra activities – such as music, sport and crafts – that may have been squeezed out of the regular school timetable, they can help to fill the gap between the end of school and the end of many parents' working day.

If you want your child to attend an after-school club, you may have a choice between one run at the school and one at a playcentre. If your child is shy or unsure of himself, he may be more comfortable staying in school, since the environment, other children and maybe the staff will be familiar. On the other hand, a club at a playcentre may give children a chance to extend themselves, and to widen their social circle.

Starting an after-school club

If your child's school doesn't have an after-school club, you might want to suggest they start one. It's a fairly big step for a school to take from scratch, so you'll need to be sure there's wide support for it – you can probably make a good start just by chatting to the other parents. While you're at it, you might check that there's no provision at a nearby playcentre – you never know what you may have missed!

Assuming there isn't, and that enough other parents are interested, your next step is probably to suggest the idea to a parent governor. Bear in mind that all of the following will need to be taken into account:

- staffing (paid and voluntary)
- charges for the use of the space (some councils have strange budgeting methods …)
- clashes with other activities (particularly if the school is used for evening classes)
- payment for the caretaker and cleaners
- insurance
- first-aid cover, and other safety issues
- cost of materials and equipment.

In practice, it will probably be necessary to involve the LEA at some level or another. Making it clear that there is plenty of support from parents can only help – especially if it takes a practical form, like fundraising or volunteering.

Volunteering at after-school clubs

Most after-school clubs welcome volunteers, and some people may prefer to help out there rather than in class – the time may suit them better, or they may prefer the more informal environment and the chance to work with children without the need to actually teach them.

Many kinds of skills can be useful – sports, arts, crafts, music, drama, cooking, sewing, gardening … really, the only limits are the imagination (taking safety and budget into account) of the staff and the enthusiasm of the children.

If you decide to volunteer, it's important to remember a few things.

- The atmosphere may be more relaxed than in school, but there are still rules and limits that the children have to obey.
- The paid staff have to take final responsibility for what goes on – so the final decision about how things are handled has to be theirs, though ideally they'll take everyone's opinions into account.
- Don't play favourites – it can be hard not to like some children more than others, but you mustn't let it show. In particular, try not to favour your children over the others.
- Once you've made a commitment to show up at a certain time, stick to it. If you can't make it, let the staff know as soon as possible.
- Remember that the children don't have to be there. An after-school club should be a fun place for them – and you.

SPORTS AND OUTDOOR PURSUITS

Some schools have a real commitment to physical activities. Others have down-played them because of pressure from the Literacy Hour, Numeracy Hour, and so on. Also, some schools believe that competitive sports go against their ethos, preferring instead to stress co-operation and sharing.

You may disagree. In any case, participation in a physical activity outside school is good for your child's fitness, and can help to build self-discipline, initiative and problem-solving activities.

Obviously, it's fairly easy to take a ball down to the local park for a kick around, or organise a game of cricket or rounders. But physical activities needn't stop there, and if you don't have the skills (or maybe the time – or energy!) to teach your child yourself, there's plenty of help around.

For example, have you considered:

- swimming
- martial arts
- gymnastics
- short tennis

- go-karting
- orienteering
- mountain biking
- in-line skating
- yoga

or any one of hundreds of other physical activities?

If you're trying to find a venue or classes for your child, your best bet is probably to start by contacting your local authority. Community centres, and even local arts centres, sometimes give space to classes – particularly martial arts and yoga.

Links

For more information, try:

- The UK Sports Council **www.uksport.gov.uk/** (mostly seems to concentrate on professional sports, but may have some useful links)
- The English Sports Council **www.english.sports.gov.uk** (links to the governing bodies for many sports, plus lots of other links)
- Northern Ireland Sports Council **www.sportscouncil-ni.org.uk/**
- Scottish Sports Council **www.ssc.org.uk/** you can also e-mail library@sportscotland.org.uk for more information)
- Sports Council for Wales **www.sports-council-wales.co.uk** or you can write or phone: Welsh Sports Institute of Sport, Sophia Gardens, Cardiff CF1 9SW, Tel.: 01222 300500, Fax: 01222 300600)
- if you have a daughter, the Women's Sports Foundation **www.wsf.org.uk/** may be able to help
- finally, if you want to check what qualifications a sports teacher or coach has, you could check out the National Coaching Foundation **www.ncf.org.uk/infoserv.htm**

ART, DRAMA AND MUSIC

These three areas have all come under pressure – at least in some schools – from the National Curriculum, yet they are vital if children are to develop their creativity.

The most obvious place to start looking for classes is your local council. You may think of them as providing evening classes, but many of them also run Saturday morning workshops (often for all the family). Don't forget to check out local community art centres, too. Finally, museums often have activity days, especially in the school holidays, but sometimes at weekends as well.

Theatre Museum **www.theatremuseum.org**

The Theatre Museum, Britain's National Museum of the Performing Arts is situated in the heart of London's theatre-land, with the world's largest and most important collections relating to the British stage. The site contains all the background information on the museum and there is also the chance to participate in a virtual online play.

Art

Art isn't just about drawing – you're likely to find courses in pottery and general crafts, such as beadwork, collage and papier mâché. Many children also enjoy photography, since it allows them to make interesting images without too much practice.

Drama

In addition to checking with your local council, you may want to consider one of the many private drama schools. Stage Register (**www.stageregister.com/**) has a guide to drama schools for under-18s, but their site is currently under construction. You can e-mail them at STAGEREGISTRAR@aol.com

Music

Unlike some other kinds of classes, learning music needs at least a bit of a commitment from your child. Also, you'll need to decide what instrument they should learn, and whether you want them to learn ensemble or solo playing.

Apart from contacting your local authority, you could try looking at adverts in your local paper, library or newsagent's window for instrumental teachers in your area.

CHAPTER 9

Keeping pets

● ● ● ● ● ● ● ● ● ●

Most children benefit from having a pet of some kind – not only because they are good fun, but because they help teach self-discipline and respect for other living creatures (and, by extension, other people). Less extrovert children, in particular, may benefit from having a companion.

However, taking on an animal is a big responsibility, and can be quite expensive. Some animals can increase the chance of allergies and asthma, because they shed fur. Also, when pets die (and some small animals have very short life spans), it can be traumatic for their young owners – though this may also help them get used to the idea of death as a natural part of life.

Before you make a final decision, you should take into account:

- How much it will cost – not just the creature itself, but its bedding and, if necessary, a cage.
- Veterinary expenses – don't forget the initial cost of inoculations (and regular boosters), and spaying or neutering.
- Day-to-day costs – food, bedding, vet's bills.
- Holiday arrangements – you can take your pet with you, pay someone to come to your home to feed it, board it out, or bribe a neighbour or a relative to look after it, but one way or the other, having a pet will affect your holidays.
- Who will take responsibility for the boring bits of looking after your pet? Cages will need cleaning out. Dogs will need walking even if it's

pouring with rain and the football's on the TV… ideally, your child will do as much of the looking after as their age allows, but if they can't or won't, it's not fair to let the pet suffer.

There's a wealth of information on the web and off it to help you decide what sort of pet to have, but here are some pointers.

Pet Health Council **www.pethealthcouncil.co.uk/**

Pets can play an important role in people's lives and they are often referred to as 'one of the family'. As well as providing a constant source of enjoyment, friendship and fun, many pets thrive in a family and household environment. This is the site of the Pet Health Council, with plenty of useful advice, particularly for dog owners. There is a handy section on introducing the pet into the family, ensuring that everyone benefits from the experience.

THE PET HEALTH COUNCIL
working for healthy pets and people

The Pet Health Council (PHC) was formed in 1979 with the specific aim of promoting the health and welfare of pet animals in the interests of both pets and people. The PHC's work is supported by a panel of medical and veterinary advisors who are experts in this field.

Educational material: The PHC has a range of information leaflets offering essential advice for both current and potential pet owners.

The leaflet range currently comprises the following:

- A Guide to Insuring Your Pet
- Choosing a Pet
- Fit Not Fat
- Getting A New Puppy
- Health Benefits of Pets
- International Pet Travel
- Pets and Allergies
- Pets and The Family
- Pets Have Teeth Too
- Practical Steps for Healthy Pets
- Stressed Pets
- The Facts About Toxoplasmosis
- Worm Your Dog!

The PHC leaflets have been written in conjunction with its panel of medical and veterinary experts. They are available to everyone from members of the public, veterinary surgeries, pet care campaigns, schools and local authorities.

DOGS

Probably more children pester their parents for dogs than any other pet.

Pros:

- Dogs are great companions – if chosen wisely, dogs will really respond to you and your child.
- There are lots of activities you can take part in if you want, like obedience and agility training, which may help your child's self-confidence and self-discipline.
- Dogs are probably the easiest pet to take with you on holiday.
- There are lots of different breeds, with a wide variety of needs, so it should be possible to find one that will fit in with most households.

Cons:

- Dogs need a lot of looking after, including daily walks.
- Need training and socialising if they – and you – are to be really happy; your child may not be up to this, but the dog may bond best to the person who trains it.
- Some dogs just don't adjust to being left and can become destructive.

Which kind of dog?

Once you've decided to get a dog, your decision making has only just begun. Choosing the right kind of dog is vital. Here are some questions to answer:

- What size dog do you want? Many people think that small dogs are best around children; in fact, this isn't always the case, since some breeds of small dog are fast-moving and nippy, while some large dogs are real gentle giants. And don't forget that big dogs require a lot more food than small ones!
- How keen are you on grooming? Long-haired dogs generally require more grooming than short-haired ones, but there are exceptions – labradors can shed a lot, for example.

- How active should the dog be? Well, how much do you like walking? Also, some breeds are very active outside, but are lazy indoors – greyhounds and lurchers are a prime example. Others, like some of the terrier breeds, don't need very long walks, but demand constant attention and playtime indoors.
- How much training do you want to do? As a rough guide, the more intelligent your dog, the more training you'll need to do – and if you don't, the dog will very likely reward you by becoming destructive, (collies are notorious in this regard). It's no good assuming your child will see to it, because if they don't, you and the rest of your household will pay the price (and so will the dog, if you decide you can't keep it).

If you'd like more help choosing, try the online questionnaire at **www.purina.com**

Where to get your dog?

The very worst place to get a dog – or just about any animal – is from a pet shop or dealer. The animals they sell will almost certainly have come from a puppy farm – where they will have been bred with no regard to genetics, and raised in inhumane conditions with very little socialisation with people.

The best places to get a pedigree dog are responsible breeders, and breed-rescue associations. Even then, it would pay you to read up on your chosen breed – each one has advantages and drawbacks, and some have significant medical problems (like deafness and hip displacia), so it's worth knowing what questions to ask.

There are several specialist dog magazines that list breeders, shelters and breed rescues, and many pet shops are now part of a scheme to refer would-be owners to responsible breeders.

If you're happy with a cross-breed, do consider visiting your local animal-rescue shelter – and remember, some older dogs make fine pets. They're over that destructive puppy stage, they're probably well socialised, and they may have the rudiments of obedience training.

Battersea Dogs' Home www.dogshome.org

Registered as a Charity No. 206394
Last updated August 2000

Credits

Copyright ©The Dogs Home Battersea 1998. All rights reserved.

Most people will be familiar with the work of this charity. The site contains plenty of useful information on dogs, including health issues. There are also a few dog-related games for your amusement.

Once you've got your dog

There are three things you must do:

• get it inoculated
• get it neutered or spayed
• get it micro-chipped or tattooed, so if it gets lost it can be returned to you.

CATS

Pros:

• Cats are affectionate but independent (which means they may like cuddles, but only when they want them, not necessarily when you do).

- They are intelligent and playful.
- They are clean.
- Cats need lower maintenance than dogs, because they don't need daily walks.
- Cats are less likely to pine than dogs if left behind when you go on holiday.
- They are relatively long lived.

Cons:

- Unlike dogs, cats can't be trained much.
- They may be too independent for some children's taste – some cats think any amount of handling is the same as harassment.
- Vet expenses are about the same as a dog – quite high compared to some small animals.
- Cats shed a lot – long-haired cats need daily grooming, and even short-haired ones (and their houses) benefit from brushing two or three times a week.

Which kind of cat?

The majority of cats in Britain are 'domestic short-hairs' – moggies, in other words. They come in a wide variety of colours, including black, white, tabby, ginger and tortoiseshell, and combinations of these. Colour generally makes very little difference, but there are some things to note:

- All-white cats may be prone to deafness, so be sure to check for this when you select your pet.
- Some people think that tortoiseshell cats are more timid or stand-offish than other colours.
- Almost all ginger cats are male; almost all tortoiseshell cats are female; this is genetically linked, so be wary of ginger females and tortoiseshell tomcats, as there may be a genetic problem – and never breed from them, as it may be passed on.

- Pedigree cats are also popular, and the different breeds each have their own characteristics. Oriental breeds, such as the Siamese, tend to be thin with pointy faces, while western breeds, like the enormous Main Coon, are heavier and rounder.
- Remember that long-haired cats like Persians really do require a lot of grooming – otherwise their fur gets badly knotted and skin problems can result.

The Cats' Protection League website (**www.cats.org.uk**) contains plenty of useful information to help you choose and look after your cat.

Where to get your cat

The very worst place is a pet shop. Many pet shops buy their animals from 'kitten-farms' – centres set up specially to breed as many kittens as possible in the shortest time, without regard to the health or temperament of the animals.

Good places to find non-pedigree kittens are by word of mouth and from animal-rescue centres. You could try asking at your local vet. Many private owners also advertise kittens – generally the product of accidental breeding. Always try to see your kitten with its mother, if you can. Remember to ask if the mother has been ill or had any health problems.

If you want a pedigree cat, you'll need to find a reputable breeder. Local vets or pet shops may know of one; check in specialist magazines; or try the Cats' Protection League.

Once you've got your cat

There are three things you must do:

- get it inoculated
- get it neutered or spayed
- get it micro-chipped or tattooed, so if it gets lost it can be returned to you.

HORSES AND PONIES

Pros:

- Horses are intelligent and affectionate.
- A horse is trainable – very much a pet to do things with, rather than just play with.
- Riding is an excellent outdoor sport that will help build and maintain fitness, confidence and self-discipline.
- Going out on rides together is a great family activity.

Cons:

- A horse will need an appropriate environment – both stabling and a field.
- A horse is extremely expensive, both to buy and to maintain (not just food and vets bills, but also possibly the cost of having it stabled, and also regular farriers' visits; there may also be the cost of riding tuition to consider).
- A horse requires high maintenance – it will need feeding, grooming and exercising every day, and the stable will need cleaning out.
- Arrangements for when you go away may be hard to make.
- Horse and child may both need training.

Choosing your horse or pony

It's essential that you choose a horse or pony that is right physically and temperamentally for your child. Unless you're an expert yourself, seek as much advice from qualified sources as you can. Your local vet or farrier may be good places to start, or check the specialist magazines. You could also try your local animal sanctuary or educational farm; or contact the Pony Club.

Pony Club **www.pony-club.org.uk/**

This is the official site for the Pony Club, with useful contacts and information about buying/owning a pony.

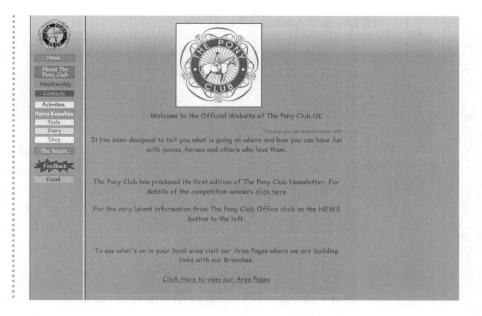

FARM ANIMALS

Some farm animals, such as goats, pigs and sheep, make surprisingly good pets. Obviously, they need a large amount of outdoor space, and aren't the best choice for city living. It's easy to get carried away by the cuteness of piglets, kids and lambs, so it's absolutely essential to get to know adult examples. City and exhibition farms are good places to visit, and can also help with advice and support. Or, as ever, try your local animal shelter.

If your child is absolutely sold on the idea of a pig or goat as a pet, and you aren't, you may be able to volunteer as a helper at a local leisure farm or animal sanctuary.

National Association of Farms for Schools
www.nfu.org.uk/nafs/

This site is devoted to the farms who host school visits, including a searchable database. Although aimed at schools, many of the farms welcome family and private visits.

SMALL MAMMALS

Small mammals such as rabbits, guinea pigs, hamsters and rats make excellent pets – though they don't tend to be terribly long-lived. This can be upsetting for some children, though it can also help them get used to the idea of death and the process of grieving, which may help them later in life.

Don't get your new hamster, rat or what have you from a pet shop – their stock often comes from farms set up to supply laboratories, and may be unhealthy or unused to humans. There are national organisations for the breeding and showing of all these animals, and they can point you in the direction of reputable breeders. Alternatively, try your local animal shelter – more small mammals need re-homing than most people would ever imagine.

All these small mammals benefit from daily handling and grooming, to get them used to people. It's possible to introduce them to cats and dogs, but be careful.

Finally, some small mammals do best in groups – but be sure they are either all the same sex or that they have been neutered, or you will have a population explosion to deal with.

Rabbits

Rabbits are one of the most popular pets in Britain – and one of the most neglected. The trouble is, people buy them, but after a while they just leave them in a little hutch at the end of the garden. Rabbits are happier roaming around, especially if the area is made more interesting with toys such as lengths of drainpipe for them to run through. Take care, though, that your garden is safe against foxes – and against bunny-turning-escape-artist!

Perhaps more surprisingly, rabbits also make good indoor pets – they can be housetrained and enjoy being cuddled and groomed. Do make sure the house is rabbit-proofed though – rodent teeth can make short work of electrical wiring (and then the wiring will make short work of the rodent …).

Rabbits are quite sociable and it's fairly common to find people keeping one with a guinea pig as a companion. However, quite often the rabbit will bully the guinea pig, so this is not necessarily to be recommended.
Useful links include:

- **www.houserabbit.co.uk**
- **www.ukpet.rabbits.org.uk/**
- **www.thewarren.demon.co.uk/**

Guinea pigs

Guinea pigs are social animals and shouldn't be kept alone – though do make sure you don't mix the sexes, or you'll have a lot of baby guinea pigs to re-home. You'll find they talk a lot and make a range of different noises, making them great fun to watch. They enjoy being handled and groomed, but need a safe place to hide away, too.
Link to **www.miju.demon.co.uk** for more information.

Rats

The poor reputation rats have is quite unfair. Tame rats are social, clean and extremely intelligent. They need company, so don't keep just one (but, as ever, separate the sexes to stop them breeding). Then you can watch their social behaviour, which is complex and fascinating. Rats respond well to handling, and can be trained.
Find out more at **www.quite.co.uk/rats/**

Hamsters

Hamsters are nocturnal – they sleep in the day and become active in the evening, when they should be fed. Several different species of hamster are kept as pets in this country. The commonest, the Syrian or golden hamster, is not at all social with its own kind, and must be kept alone. Other species of hamster can be kept in groups. All of them become friendly to humans if they are handled regularly.

Complete Hamster Site **www.hamsters.co.uk**

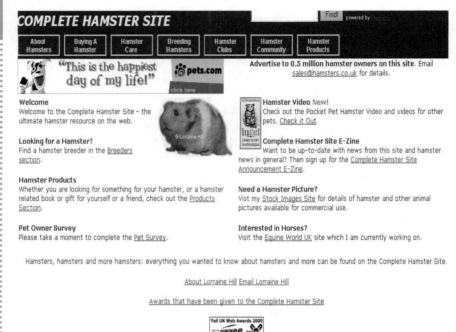

This site has everything you need to know about buying and keeping hamsters. There are also details of hamster clubs and events with which to get involved.

BIRDS

Some birds make better pets than you might expect, being surprisingly intelligent and capable of affection if handled regularly and with care. As ever, go to a reputable breeder or your local animal shelter, rather than a pet shop.

Budgerigars

Budgerigars are small, and can be kept inside in a reasonably sized cage, though they will also thrive outside in suitable aviary. They are reasonably cheap to maintain and are probably amongst the easiest pets to find holiday-care for. They are excellent mimics, though they learn to talk best when kept alone. Otherwise, they'll appreciate the company of other birds, since they live in flocks in the wild.

www.budgerigarsociety.com/ can tell you all you need to know.

Parrots

Parrots are extremely intelligent, so they need a lot of stimulation. Some species can live to 80 or more, so a parrot is a long-term commitment. That said, one might make an interesting pet for an older child interested more in training and learning about their pet than in cuddles!

www.theparrotsocietyuk.org/ can tell you more about parrots, parakeets and related birds.

Other birds

Many species of small birds, such as lovebirds, canaries and mynah birds, are available as pets. As with all animals, it's best to seek expert advice before you commit yourself to taking one on. Be especially careful that any bird you buy has been bred in captivity and not caught in the wild – the death-rate for imported birds is enormous.

Though not British, **www.petstation.com/** has a large number of links to British foreign bird clubs.

REPTILES

Reptiles as pets are probably more interesting than cute or cuddly.

Tortoises

These slow-moving animals can live up to 150 years and it's possible that one you buy will be older than your child – if not you.

Tortoises are vegetarian, and will enjoy roaming (slowly!) around your garden, browsing as they go. However, don't let their speed, or lack of it, fool you. Some tortoises are great escape artists, so you'll need secure fencing.

There are strict laws against importing tortoises, so it's imperative that you get yours from a reputable source. It's also extremely important that you understand how to care for it, and especially how to help it to prepare for hibernation.

Check out **www.tortoisetrust.org/** for more information, or try **www.britishcheloniagroup.org.uk/**

Terrapins

Terrapins are essentially aquatic, carnivorous tortoises. They can be very pretty, but although they start out small – they can grow huge. Their tanks can get extraordinarily smelly, even if they're cleaned out daily, because they eat meat in the water. Generally, terrapins don't make good pets unless you are very committed to them.

Find out what's involved at **www.tortoisetrust.org/**

Snakes

Snakes are fascinating, and despite their reputation, not at all slimy! You should seek expert advice before you decide to get one as a pet, and as always, get your snake from a reputable breeder or from an animal sanctuary rather than buying from a pet shop.

The snakes kept as pets are generally constrictors – that is, non-poisonous. They are perfectly safe to handle, though allowing one to coil round your neck is not recommended. Some species, such as corn snakes are better for beginners than others, though you should, of course, seek expert advice. They will need a vivarium (tank) with 24-hour heating, so they can be a bit expensive to keep. They will also need to be fed with dead chicks or baby mice every few days. You can buy these frozen from pet shops, but it may not be a job for the squeamish.

Try **www.nafcon.dircon.co.uk/index.html** if you're still interested.

Lizards

Lizards are difficult to care for well, and are probably not the best choice for children or beginners. That said, if you'd like to know more, try **www.nafcon.dircon.co.uk/index.html**

INSECTS AND OTHER ANIMALS

Yes, people really do keep insects as pets! **www.ex.ac.uk/bugclub/** can tell you all you need to know.

Spiders

The spiders most commonly kept as pets are tarantulas such as the Chilean Rose. They don't bite, but their hairs can be extremely irritating. Such spiders are not a particularly good choice as children's pets.

Stick Insects

Stick insects are easy to keep – they just need a glass tank filled with the right kind of greenery. They aren't cuddly and they don't really do that much, but they're still fun to watch (and a great way to play a live game of 'Where's Wally?').

Other animals

It's also possible to keep snails and caterpillars – including silkworms. Or check out Parents Online's guide (**www.parents.org.uk**) to making a wormery.

CHAPTER 10

Parties

● ● ● ● ●

If there's one thing more exciting and nerve-wracking than your birthday party when you're a child, it's surely being the adult responsible for it.

Basically, there are three phases to any party – preparing for it, running it, and clearing up afterwards. Of these, preparing is arguably the most important – or at least the thing with the most potential for saving your nerves!

PREPARING A PARTY

First, set a budget. From this, everything else flows. Remember you'll need money for:

- invitations
- food
- decorations (possibly including table cloths etc.)
- prizes for games
- perhaps to hire an entertainer (*see* page 117).

Next, decide whether you want to invite as many children as you can, or spend more per head. If that sounds easy, be warned – it can be a minefield of hurt feelings. Be careful not to exclude children who might reasonably expect an invitation. With primary class sizes running at 30 or more, it can be difficult to invite an entire class – you may have to hope that your child has a well defined circle of friends. Don't forget that you might want to invite some children from outside school – from the after-school club, or Brownies, or gym class or whatever.

Make sure you can rope people in to help – not just on the day, but with preparations and cleaning up, too.

Decide whether or not to have a theme, or split the difference and have a non-themed fancy dress party. Obviously, the time of year may influence your choices. Good themes include 'Into Space', 'Hallowe'en', 'The Night Before Christmas', 'The Magician's Castle', 'The Wizard of Oz', 'At the Zoo', 'Racing Cars', etc. Choose something with plenty of scope for dressing up and room decorations. You and your helpers might consider dressing up, too.

Room decorations can be as simple or as complicated as you like. For instance, for a space theme, you could fix large sheets of black paper to the walls (use Blu-Tack or some other non-permanent method), then cut out the shapes of rockets, stars and planets, comets and so on from silver foil, and stick them to the paper. The only limit, really, is your imagination.

Try to keep one room child-free, so the adults can take it in turns to sneak off somewhere quiet – great for fraying nerves!

FOOD

Try to provide something nutritious to begin with. If you're concerned that children will go only for the sweet gooey stuff, put out the more substantial food before you let them see the goodies.

You can have a lot of fun matching food to the theme of the party. It needn't be too difficult – it's amazing what you can do with a set of pastry cutters and a few bottles of food dye. You could also make themed labels for the food (these aren't fairy cakes, they're Plutonian chocolate bombs …). (You'll find lots of interesting recipes at **www.parents.org.uk**. Many of these are Hallowe'en themed, but it shouldn't be too difficult to adapt them.)

Don't forget to dress the table appropriately – it could be great fun for each child to have a 'rocket ship control panel' place mat, along with a 'starship Identification Card place marker', for example.

On a practical note, you might want to use paper plates, cups, and table cloths – or compromise and use wipeable plastic cloths. This definitely isn't a time for the best linen and fine china. Try to clean up as you go – even just dumping rubbish into bin bags, and scraping dishes and putting them into soak will help no end.

FUN AND GAMES

Make sure you have some small treats to give away as prizes. Lots of games need music, so make sure you buy a suitable CD or tape, or choose tracks from different CDs and put them all on one tape.

Here are reminders of some the old favourite games, and some new ones too.

- **Pass the parcel** – give the old favourite a new twist by putting sweets between some of the layers of paper; use a pretty sheet of paper every so often so that people think they've found the middle when they haven't.
- **Musical bumps** – easier to arrange than musical chairs. When the music stops, everyone sits on the floor. Last child sitting is 'out'.
- **Statues** – everyone skips around or dances. When the music stops, they freeze. Anyone spotted moving is 'out'.
- **Balloon racer** – the children divide into teams and line up. Give each team a balloon. The first person has to hold the balloon under her chin and pass it to the next person without using her hands. If the balloon bursts, the team can have a new one, but it starts at the front again. The first team to get the balloon all the way down the line wins.
- **Balloon relay** – the teams line up; the first person passes the balloon through his legs to the next person, and so on. When the last person gets the balloon, he races to the front with it and hands it to the next person. Then he sits down. The first team to get everyone sitting down wins.
- **Rice racing** – this is best played on a hard floor. Each child has a straw and a grain of uncooked rice. They hold the straw in their mouth and use it to push the rice along. The first person to the finish line wins.
- **Pinata** – this is an old Spanish/American Christmas tradition, but you can adapt it for use any time. You'll need a large box (not too sturdy, or you'll be there all night). Cover it with pretty paper and fill it with sweets and confetti. Attach a string and tie it to the branch of

a tree, or the frame of an open door. Children take turns to be blindfolded and whack the pinata with a stick. Be warned – when it breaks and the sweets fall out, there's generally a free-for-all.

- **Pin the tail on the donkey** – adapt the picture to match your theme.
- **Scavenger hunt** – make a list of things for children to find. These should be a mixture of easy and hard to find. Be sure to set limits as to where children can and can't go, and be certain they know what they are. First person (or team) to get back with all the objects wins a prize.
- **Hunt the space monster/witch's cat etc.**– like hunt the thimble, but adapted to fit your theme.
- **Treasure hunt** – prepare this well in advance. Write clues that lead to each other and hide them around the house and garden. The final clue either leads to a prize, or you (and then you give out a prize). Team the children up so that everyone is with a good reader.
- **Sleepy lions** – the best way to calm them all down at the end of the day, but do match it to your theme if you can. Everyone lies down on the floor and stays as still as possible. The first sleepy lion to twitch is 'out' and has to come and help you watch the others.

TIME TO GO HOME

Make sure your child says goodbye to each friend as they leave. It's nice to give each one a small goody bag on the way out, but try not to let it get out of hand. A few sweets, perhaps a small toy or a comic is quite enough.

Cleaning up

You might be tempted to leave the mess. Don't be. You'll only regret it in the morning. Make sure you've got plenty of strong bin bags and simply sweep all the rubbish into them – this is where those paper cups and plates come into their own.

And then … relax! You've done it!

CHAPTER 11

Leisure tips

● ● ● ● ● ● ● ● ●

Long hot summer days and rainy winter afternoons both provide the same challenge – how to entertain your children. Here are some ideas for you to use and adapt:

IN AN HOUR OR TWO

- Read a book together, then make up a new ending for the story.
- Play a game on your computer.
- Write a letter to a friend you haven't seen for a long time.
- Play a board game.
- Play a story-telling game – one person starts, and stops at a cliffhanger. The next person has to get the hero out of trouble!
- Draw or paint a picture – either from your imagination, or set up a few interesting objects, look really closely and draw what you can see.
- Decide where you'll go on the next sunny day – what can you find out about it on the web?

OnlineWeather **www.onlineweather.com**

In the UK the weather seems to rule our lives: not only do we spend all our time talking about it, but with children it can make or break a family day out. This site is invaluable, providing seemingly accurate four-day forecasts in a simple-to-understand format. If on holiday or travelling, OnlineWeather will provide forecasts for most major UK towns and cities. If abroad, the site provides links to most local equivalents.

- Play old-fashioned games like the Parson's Cat. ('The Parson's Cat is an amiable cat …'; the next person repeats that, and adds an adjective starting with 'b', and so on … Can you get all the way through the alphabet without missing a letter or forgetting a word?)
- Collect items to make a 'time capsule' – what will you choose to tell the future about your life?
- Try a craft project like leaf printing or making paper flowers – you'll find plenty of ideas on the Parents Online website (**www.parents.org.uk**).
- Make a weather station to put outside when the weather clears up.
- Do some cooking together.

Cooking with Kids **www.cookingwithkids.com**

This site contains excerpts from *Cooking with Kids for Dummies*, additional tips and recipes, fun and games, links to other kids' cooking sites, plus 'The Peppered Leopard kids' area.

- Drape a blanket over a clothes airer to make a shop, a tent, a space capsule …
- Play at dressing up – any old clothes will do, the more outrageous the better!
- Make paper airplanes and see which one flies best.

Alex's Paper Airplanes **www.paperairplanes.co.uk**

This site contains a comprehensive selection of designs for paper airplanes, including accurate folding instructions. Each design includes an overview to its flying characteristics and is usefully ranked by difficulty to build.

- Go to the library.
- Go swimming.
- Create an internet treasure hunt: devise a list of questions (examples at **www.parents.org.uk** that follow some sort of pattern, then find the answers on the web.
- If it's hot and you've got a garden (and there isn't a ban!) get the hosepipe out and play at waterfights – or fill a paddling pool and make paper boats to float.
- Picnic in the garden instead of having lunch indoors.
- Go for a good long walk, or a cycle ride.
- Get a group of children together and go to the park to play games – take a ball and play football or netball, or check out the Parents Online website for games to play with groups of kids (**www,parents.org.uk**).
- Play French cricket or rounders in the garden, or get the swingball out.
- Look for minibeasts – insects, spiders, snails – in the garden. Make puppets based on them (instructions on the Parents Online website).

- Take a picnic to the park.
- Make a wormery – see the instructions at **www.parents.org.uk**
- Play old-games like 'What's the time Mr Wolf?' and Grandmother's footsteps.
- Teach your dog a new trick – or if you don't know how, find a good obedience class. You could even consider teaching him agility or flyball.
- Find a pond with some ducks and feed them.
- Make a puppet theatre out of a sheet and a clothes airer, and puppets out of stiff card and lollypop sticks.
- Make up a story and write it down – you could make a book yourself (sew or staple sheets of paper together) – then illustrate it. Using word processing and drawing packages and use your computer to help with the production of the book.
- Set up camp in the garden – if it's warm, sleep out overnight (but still use a sleeping bag and tent). Eat sausages, beans and baked potatoes (cooked indoors) and pretend to be in the Old West. Or send for take-away pizza – it'll never taste so good.
- Paint a white tee-shirt with fabric paint, or tie it up with string and dye it for an authentic 1970s retro look. Or, for a child-friendly way of making batik, draw designs on the shirt with the end of a candle (you'll need to push really hard to get enough wax – you can also try using crayons), then dye it; when it's dry, iron it between several sheets of brown paper to get rid of the wax.
- Make a kite and fly it.
- Visit a pet show – maybe even enter your pet!
- Knit or sew something.
- Put on a play and make costumes out of dressing-up clothes, tea towels or crêpe paper.

IN A DAY

Visit Britain **www.visitbritain.com**

This site provided by the British Tourist Authority is the official travel guide to Britain. Enter the site by selecting where you are coming from (don't forget to click the arrow under the box after selecting). A customised site, in your native language, is then presented to you. The home page presents you with an interactive map of the UK which will allow you to progressively work down to street level. Information is organised in categories such as Accommodation, Destinations to Visit, Attractions, Activities and Events. There are a variety of suggestions for holidays and tours and emphasis on various age groups, including links to **www.uktheguide.com** with a focus on young Britain. There is also infuriation on the National Accessible Scheme for travellers with disabilities.

- Find a child-friendly museum to visit. Be sure to find out if they have children's activities or fun worksheets to do.
- Go to the zoo.

Eventselector **www.eventselector.co.uk/**

Children these days seem to be much more sophisticated and expectations are much higher when it comes to leisure activities. For parents trying to meet these requirements it is quite a challenge. Eventselector allows you to search 'What's On Guides' across the country. It's the sort of information you would find in your local paper but with the added benefit of covering a wide range of activities. The site covers cinema, theatre and arts, and has a special kids section – very useful during the holidays.

Also covered is a TV guide for the week ahead, which is great for helping you plan what to watch and programmes to avoid with the children.

• Plan a trip to the nearest big city, and choose two or three tourist attractions to visit (or more if you – and your child – have the stamina!)

Multimap www.multimap.com

For days out and finding how to get to your friends, Multimap is an excellent site. As the name suggests, this site is all about maps, covering the whole of Great Britain to street level. Multimap makes the most of the internet and demonstrates how the technology can be applied to everyday applications. It is possible to search by a variety of methods, including post-code, street name, place name and grid reference. The site then presents a map at street level – very useful as most of us will only have a local street map. If required you can then zoom out and/or link to other details such as accommodation.

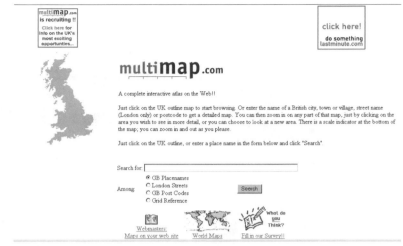

- Visit an exhibition farm.
- Go for a drive in the country – or find a bus tour.

NFU Countryside www.nfucountryside.org.uk

This is the public face of the National Farmers' Union: a site for anyone interested in the countryside. If you enjoy visiting the country there is a useful events calendar, including details of all the county shows. Children will enjoy the Friendly Farm Club, which features games and animated stories.

- Go to the cinema. Find out what's on by looking up **www.uci-cinemas.co.uk**, **www.virgin.net/cinema** or **www.odeon.co.uk**
- Find a country house with interesting things for children to do.

5 minutesaway www.5minutesaway.co.uk

If you dread long car journey with miserable children, this is the site for you. Using a clear graphical interface you can navigate your way around the major motorways, locating facilities within five minutes of each junction. The site contains a directory listing of 1500 pubs, restaurants, petrol stations, leisure spots and shops. This would be a great site to use when planning that long holiday trip.

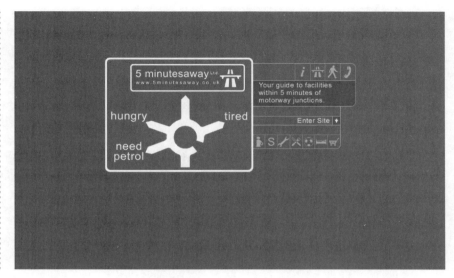

- Visit a wildlife centre that has open days – you might find one where you can see birds of prey, for example.
- Go horseriding.
- Go fishing.
- See if your local sports team does an open day or behind-the-scenes tour.
- Go to the theatre – a children's show or a musical, perhaps. Or at Christmas, of course, there's the pantomime (see www.parents.org.uk for a panto guide).
- Get tickets for a TV or radio show (contact the BBC or your local independent stations).
- Visit a funfair or fête.
- Go to an art gallery – but do your research first (find one with interesting pictures and sculptures; don't be afraid to talk about what you're looking at; and choose just a few exhibits to look at so you leave while your child is still having a good time).
- Keep an eye out for open days at your local fire and police stations.
- Hire a boat on a lake or canal.
- Take a camera out (a disposable one will do if you haven't already got one) and see what you can find to take pictures of.

IN TWO DAYS OR MORE

Even if you've only got a weekend, you can still get away. The longer the trip, the more carefully you should plan. Try to find somewhere that offers things to do even if the weather isn't great. Going away on impulse is great fun, and you may pick up a bargain, but the best savings – and the greatest choice – are made when you book well in advance.

• For minimal hassle, go to a hotel or bed-and-break-fast – but check that children are welcome first.

WWW

LeisureHunt www.leisurehunt.com

This is an impressive and ambitious site that taps into vast accommodation data from around the world. By entering either a post-code or town name, the site will list accommodation details in the locality. Using mapping technology the site calculates how far each site is from your requested point, If required this then links to a local map. Although mainly focused on hotels, self-catering accommodation is also handled. The site also allows you to find leisure attractions, pubs and restaurants for each search location.

- If you're on a budget, consider self-catering – though if that means you're going to eat out at every meal, it may not work out cheaper after all. You might want to think about renting somewhere atmospheric – it's possible to stay in castles, inns and follies.

Recommended Cottages
www.recommended-cottages.co.uk

Another popular family holiday is country cottages. This site allows you to search a database of over 500 properties. Criteria for searching includes area, number of bedrooms and people in your party. Full details on each property are given and also availability. If required you can then use the online-booking facility. Finally, the site brings extra value to the whole holiday planning process by providing details of attractions local to each cottage.

- Camping is fun, healthy and cheap – but you may want to try it when the weather's at it's best.

Camping www.camping.org.uk

Camping is a fantastic family activity and for many a great hobby throughout the year. With modern equipment, camping can even be quite luxurious. This site is the online equivalent of the many popular camp site directories and guides. Of course, being electronic brings the usual benefits of being able to search by a variety of criteria, including a particular area/region of a country and the facilities a site can offer. For families it is therefore very easy to find the sites with that essential feature of a heated indoor swimming pool. For those who cannot quite face the complete outdoor life, many sites offer luxury lodges and other similar accommodation to rent.

- You could also hire a caravan (either static or to tow), or try a boat on the Norfolk Broads or one of the canals.

Consider going somewhere a bit different – whatever that means to you. For example, you could:

- Stay on a farm.

Farm Holidays www.farm-holidays.co.uk

A site representing over a 1000 farms providing both bed-and-break-fast and self-catering accommodation throughout the UK, in quality accommodation with value-for-money prices.

- Take the children abroad (the Channel Tunnel means France has never been so accessible (**www.eurostar.co.uk** and **www.eurotunnel.co.uk**)).
- Go to the Lake District or the Peaks.
- Explore the legend of King Arthur in the West Country.
- Go fossil hunting (the Isle of Wight is great for this).

Fossil collecting
www.web.ukonline.co.uk/conker/fossils/

A site devoted to fossil collecting.

- Go bird watching. (**www.rspb.org.uk**)
- Take a course – many study centres welcome children, and it's nothing like being at school!
- Go pony trekking or walking on the moors.
- Visit some of the Scottish islands.
- Or you could even consider sending your children off on an adventure holiday by themselves …

The British Activity Holiday Association website has links to many companies that provide holidays for accompanied children and families (**www.baha.org.uk/**).

SEASONAL ACTIVITIES

General activities are all very well, but certain times of the year demand special attention.

Winter

- Take advantage of the long nights to get out in the country and really look at the sky – find out which constellations are which, and how they got their names. Look up the Hubble Space Telescope website at **http://oposite.stsci.edu/pubinfo/pictures.html** to view some stunning images from space.
- Walks in winter have their own magic – especially in the woods. Get out early if you can, and take a camera with you.
- If it snows, go out and look for animal footprints.

- Make a cat-and-squirrel-proof bird table (but if you start feeding the birds, don't just stop – they grow to depend on it). Can you identify all the birds that visit? Can you provide particular foods to attract certain birds?

Christmas

- Visit Santa's grotto at the department store of your choice.
- Write a letter to Father Christmas – and read *The Father Christmas Letters* by J.R.R. Tolkien. Other great Christmas books include Raymond Briggs's *The Snowman* and Antonia Barber and Nicola Bayley's *The Mousehole Cat.*

Christmas www.christmas.com

This site is sure to impress. Christmas.com has plenty of pages to help you prepare for the festive season, even a countdown to worry you over the number of days left. There are the usual suggestions for gifts, as well as the chance to create your own wish-lists to mail to friends and family. The site includes an extensive games area, including a Christmas crossword. If you dread the office party there are plenty of hints and tips to survive the event and secure your job for the new year.

- Go to a pantomime.
- Make your own cards, Christmas decorations and gift boxes – you'll find plenty of help on the Parents Online website (**www.parents.org.uk**).
- Make mince pies.
- Decorate the Christmas tree.
- Go carol singing.

Christmas carols **www.christmas-time.com**

This site contains a selection of Christmas carols, complete with lyrics and tunes. The site also includes plenty of Christmas-related content.

- Even if you aren't Christian, investigate the Christmas story and its pagan predecessors.
- Don't buy a pet – it's the very worst time of year.

New Year's Eve

- Make a 'time capsule' and bury or hide it (for full instructions see the Parents Online Website at **www.parents.org.uk**).
- Find all the words to 'Auld Lang Syne' – and work out what they mean.

Kids Jokes **www.kidsjokes.co.uk**

Children love jokes. This UK site contains several thousand clean, fun jokes for children of all ages. The site is divided up into lots of categories: knock-knock jokes, animal jokes, school jokes and more.

Spring

- Give your child a garden patch and help them work out what to plant.
- Decorate your child's bedroom and let them help with the colour scheme. Find simple things they can help with, like stripping wallpaper or stamping designs on the wall.
- If it's a good hot spring, swap the birdtable for a bird bath.
- Spring is a good time to make sure your children are confident in the water, before the summer holidays come around, so take them swimming.

Valentine's Day

- Make your own cards and paper flowers.
- Make chocolate crispies or other sweets as gifts.
- Find out who St Valentine was.

Easter

- Make an Easter bonnet (directions on the Parents Online website).

Easter www.holidays.net/easter

This site is a celebration of Easter with historical and religious backgrounds to this holiday. You can also find out the history of the Easter

Bunny. There are the usual recipes and Easter pictures for children to print out and colour. A useful starting point when discussing Easter.

- Make pancakes – and be sure to flip them!
- Hide mini Easter eggs all over the house and garden – write clues or just let your children tear the place apart looking for them.

British Eggs www.eggsedu.org.uk

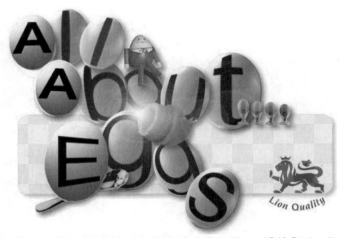

Welcome to All About Eggs; an exciting educational web site for pupils aged 5-16. Produced in consultation with teachers and educationalists, All About Eggs offers a wealth of fun and inspiring resources, recipes, and eggy information for teachers, parents and students.

All About Eggs is produced in association with
The British Egg Information Service (BEIS)

Enter

Developed by SkillsWare and EPR

This is the educational site for the British Egg Information Service. It includes several schools projects across all ages and a recipe game. For Easter there are plenty of egg-based activities, including recipes, art and science.

- Visit a local wildlife centre to see the newborn animals.
- Even if you aren't Christian, investigate the Easter story and its pagan predecessors.

Summer

- Make the most of the long days by getting out as much as you can.
- Find out about Midsummer – the longest day of the year – and the legends that surround it.
- If you've never been camping, now's the best time to start.
- Collect flowers (but not wildflowers, unless you really know what you're doing – many of them are protected by law) to dry or make into pot pourri.

Greenfingers www.greenfingers.com

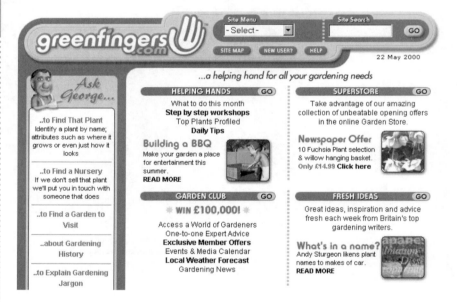

This is a big site devoted to gardening. For families there is plenty on offer, including online gardening workshops. Also of interest is the 'Plant Finder', a database of thousands of types, which, by asking key questions, allows you to discover the name of that plant at the bottom of the garden.

Autumn

- Collect leaves and use them for printing (instructions on the Parents Online website).

- Use up spare fruit by cooking it – pies and tarts are more child-friendly that jams and pickles.
- In late autumn, plant bulbs in pots and bowls ready for Christmas (instructions on the Parents Online website).
- Make your own candles ready for Hallowe'en, Guy Fawkes and Christmas (close parental supervision is an absolute must).

Hallowe'en

- Carve a jack o'lantern out of a big pumpkin and put a nightlight inside.
- Paint your children's faces, dress them up, and take them out trick-or-treating, American style. Remember to have sweets at home in case you get any visitors!
- Cut silhouettes of witches, cats, and ghosts out of black paper and stick them on the window – you can make moons and stars out of silver foil; but if your child is prone to nightmares, better make it the frontroom window, not the one in the bedroom!
- *The Nightmare Before Christmas* is a great Hallowe'en movie, but might be too scary for the littlest children. The *Meg and Mog* picture books might be a better bet.

Guy Fawkes Night

- Check up on the Fireworks Code – and make sure your children know it as well as you do. (You'll find web links on page 117.)
- Go to a public fireworks display for maximum safety. If you must have fireworks or a bonfire at home, make safety your top priority.
- Sausages, baked potatoes with beans, and kebabs in pitta bread are all great bonfire-night food – whether or not you have a bonfire!
- Find out who Guy Fawkes was and why he ends up on the bonfire every year.
- Make firework pictures by rubbing different colours of crayons thickly on black paper. Then paint over them with black paint – scratch through to reveal random colours.

BEST INTERACTIVE WEBSITES

BBC www.bbc.co.uk

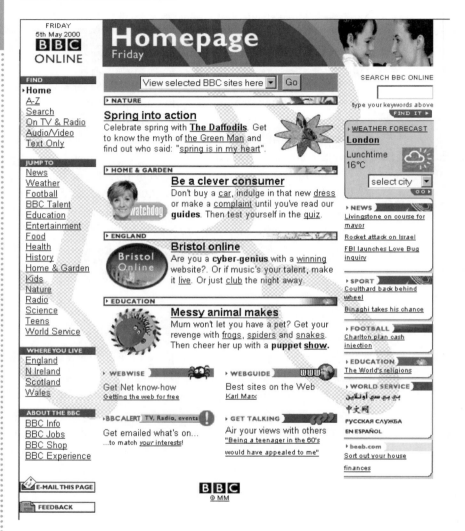

This is a huge and ever-changing site. It has the benefit of continuous promotion by BBC Television and is very popular. We recommend you locate and bookmark your favourite areas, so you can navigate back to them easily. Here are a few suggestions.

Parenting **www.bbc.co.uk/health/parenting**

We could call this site 'How to be a parent and smile the whole time'. There's advice not just on parenting but also preparing for parenthood throughout the pregnancy, illnesses, baby's needs and your needs. Produced in collaboration with the Health Education Authority, this site is a must for every parent-to-be. Helpful topics include techniques for coping with a newborn baby, dealing with bedwetting, tantrums and tempers, common childhood illnesses and accidents and immunising your child against fatal illnesses. Contact details are provided for a wide variety of support groups and organisations.

Children's BBC **www.bbc.co.uk/kids**

This is the supporting site for Children's BBC (CBBC), containing sub-sites for all the key TV programmes including that old favourite *Blue Peter*. These sites contain plenty of activities, puzzles, games and competitions. Through the use of the internet, children now can become involved and participate with their favourite programmes, rather than passively watch TV.

Shockwave **www.shockwave.com**

Shockwave has become the standard for adding interaction to websites. It is basically a plug-in that allows developers to bring a website to life. Many sites use Shockwave to offer games and other interactive devices. Shockwave.com is the mother site for all this interaction, where you can access some of the best movies. These cover entertainment and educational offerings, complete with a searchable database. A popular game with children is Lego Snap, where you have to match cards of animals. A correct result plays a sound effect of the relevant animal.

Aardman Animations **www.aardman.com**

Wallace and Gromit have been family favourites for some time. Here you will find the official site. You can find out all about the characters and the various films. There is a wealth of background detail about how the films are produced, including some of the working sketches showing how the animations are produced. You can download some of those famous sound bites such as 'Don't forget the crackers'. There are some neat games to play and you can even help Wallace in his workshop with some of those whacky inventions. The site also showcases much of Aardman's other work and gives you the chance to see sample movie clips.

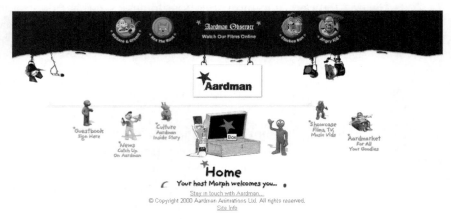

Bonus.com **www.bonus.com**

This massive sites holds over 1000 games from arcade action to classic board games. Although the site's main aim is entertainment, many of the games include educational elements. Many games originate from the US, which shouldn't mar their enjoyment, but look out for spelling and currency differences.

Disney **www.disney.co.uk**

Every family will be familiar with Disney and this lavish site has much to offer. Here you will find details of all your favourite characters and films, Disney parks and other products. There are loads of online games and pictures to colour, all featuring Disney characters

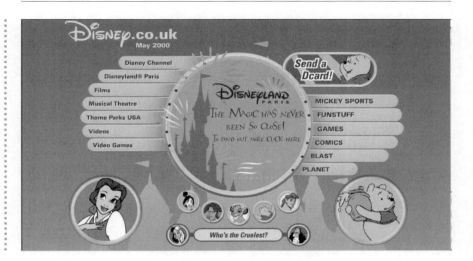

CHAPTER 12

Health

● ● ● ● ●

The world wide web is a treasure house of information; it's available 24 hours a day, seven days a week; and no matter how obscure or embarrassing your complaint, it will never make you blush. All in all, it's not surprising that more and more people are turning to the web for medical advice.

MEDICAL INFORMATION ON THE WEB

There's a downside, though. No web page can substitute for a knowledgeable doctor (especially not one who knows you well) and very few web pages are guaranteed reliable and up-to-date. It follows that you should treat medical information you find on the web with caution – perhaps more as a way of researching something before a visit to the doctor than as a solution in itself, or as a way of finding out about alternative therapies like acupuncture or homeopathy.

If you're really worried about something and you can't get to your GP's surgery, remember that you can always phone NHS Direct (0845 4647). If you have a real medical emergency (such as chest or stomach pains, or a suspected fracture), then you should phone for an ambulance.

NHS Direct **www.nhsdirect.nhs.uk**

This site describes itself as your gateway to health information on the internet. It includes the NHS 'A–Z guide', which is a database originally commissioned as part of the implementation of the Patient's Charter and has now been converted for internet access. The database covers issues such as NHS funding and organisation, how to get access to services when you need them, how to complain and make suggestions, and how to get help from other services, including benefits, social services, residential care, etc. The site also gives details of NHS Direct, the 24-hour nurse-led free telephone advice and information service.

Patient UK **www.patient.org.uk**

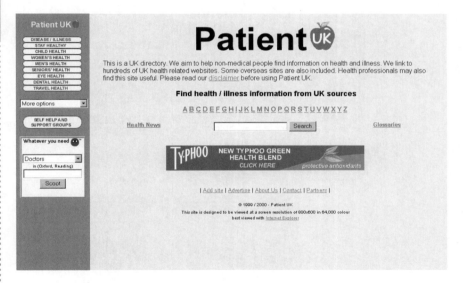

This is a UK directory intended to help non-medical people find information on health and illness (health professionals may also find this site useful). It links to hundreds of UK health-related websites. Some overseas sites are also included. There are various ways of navigating around the information. There are individual sections on women's, men's and child health and a section on health issues associated with travelling. A variety of links are given to self-help and support groups and there is an integrated 'Scoot' search facility to help you locate healthcare facilities in your area.

Netdoctor **www.netdoctor.co.uk**

Although the internet cannot turn parents into medical experts, the ability to search quickly health databases may provide initial advice before calling the doctor. Netdoctor offers a comprehensive medical database with a special children's section. Most common diseases are included, with links to other external sources. A special online diagnostic section allows you to test yourself in certain conditions. But, as always, you should consult the experts.

National Meningitis Trust **www.meningitis-trust.org.uk**

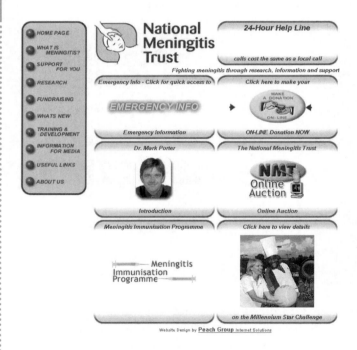

Meningitis is probably one of the most worrying of diseases for parents, because of its killer nature and prevalence with children. This site provides plenty of useful background and support. One of the most frightening aspects of Meningitis is its speed of attack and the difficulty of detecting the symptoms, which often mirror those of more common illnesses. It is here that the web really scores, providing quick facts to help you diagnose some of the symptoms. As with all sites covering such important information, you should only treat them as guidance and always consult a doctor if you have any doubt.

Autism Initiatives **www.autism-initiatives.co.uk**

Autism is a dysfunction of the brain that disrupts the development of social, communication and imagination skills, isolating those it affects from the rest of us. Although this site is aimed at support activities within the North West, there is plenty of general advice and background on autism. Of particular interest will be the top-ten suggestions of how to visualise everyday life.

Dyspraxia **www.emmbrook.demon.co.uk/dysprax/homepage.htm**

Dyspraxia is an immaturity of the brain resulting in messages not being properly transmitted to the body. This site covers plenty of background and practical advice on dyspraxia. Interestingly, there is a section dedicated to contributions from children with dyspraxia. In their own words, the children illustrate some of problems they experience.

Contact a Family **www.cafamily.org.uk**

Helping families who care for children with any disability or special need

Contact a Family

Every day over sixty children in the UK are born or diagnosed with a serious disability and the vast majority of them are cared for at home. Contact a Family (CaF) is the **only** UK charity providing support and advice to parents whatever the medical condition of their child.

Discovering that your child has a special need or disability is probably one of the most devastating experiences that a parent will live through. The feeling of isolation - both physically and emotionally - can often be acute. However, experience tells us that some of this pain can be relieved by sharing thoughts and fears with other families in a similar situation. We have information on over 1,000 rare syndromes and rare disorders and can put families in touch with each other.

[More Information] [The CaF Directory of Specific Conditions and Rare Disorders]
[The Rare Disorders Alliance - UK] [Accesskeys] [Site Map] [Site Statistics]

Contact a Family, 170 Tottenham Court Road, London W1P 0HA
Tel 020 7383 3555 .... Fax.020 7383 0259

e-mail: info@cafamily.org.uk

Registered Charity Number 284912

Every day over 60 children in the UK are born or diagnosed with a serious disability and the vast majority of them are cared for at home. Contact a Family (CaF) is the only UK charity providing support and advice to parents whatever the medical condition of their child. This site has comprehensive details on over 1000 rare syndromes and rare disorders and can put families in touch with each other.

Trashed www.trashed.co.uk

Trashed is one of the many sites to come out of the Health Education Authority (HEA) addressing individual health issues. This site is devoted to drugs and contains plenty of useful information across many substances. Background information is given on the effects, risks and what to do in an emergency, and is presented as a separate page for each drug.

Child dental care www.mclean1953.freeserve.co.uk/

Getting the children to brush their teeth twice a day seems to be one of those eternal battles for most parents. This site was created by a parent after their young child developed tooth decay. They had less sugar in their diet than most children, visited a dentist regularly, brushed twice a day with fluoride toothpaste and had been told their teeth were fine at the last dental visit. British dentists were unhelpful in providing information so they had to do their own literature searches. The site provides plenty of background information, including tips on how to get the children to brush their teeth regularly.

ChildLine www.childline.org.uk

This is the site for the well-known children's charity, the UK's free national helpline for children and young people in trouble or danger. The site is usefully split for children and adults, allowing the different audiences to be catered for in an appropriate manner. For children, there are a number of role-playing scenarios to follow. For adults there is a range of helpful fact sheets including : 'Bereavement', 'Bullying',

'Child abuse', 'Suicide', 'HIV/AIDS', 'Stepfamilies', 'Exam stress', and 'Eating problems'. There are also details of ChildLine's schools programme, CHIPS.

National Asthma Campaign **www.asthma.org.uk/**

Asthma seems to be a growing problem of modern life. Although it is not necessarily caused by our lifestyle, that is certainly considered to be a contributing factor. This is the official site of the National Asthma Campaign charity. The site contains plenty of background information on asthma and appropriate advice. There is also a self-help plan for you to download and follow in conjunction with your doctor. Asthma is far more prelevant in children, with one in seven affected (over three times the incidence in adults). Accordingly there is a children's club to encourage their involvement and understanding.

Glossary

Glossary

• • • • • •

Action Plan A school's response to the report made by the Registered Inspector after an OFSTED inspection. It must be prepared within 40 working days of the report being received, and made available to all parents.

Attainment target The knowledge, skills and understanding your child must learn at each level of the National Curriculum.

Core subject English, mathematics or science – the three subjects that children must study between the ages of 5 and 16, and in which they take the SATs. In Wales, Welsh may be studied as a core subject.

Ethos (of school) The atmosphere and environment of the school, including the way it expects children and staff to behave towards each other, and how the school interacts with the wider community.

Failing (school) A school that an OFSTED inspection decides is not providing an adequate standard of education.

Foundation Stage The earliest phase of education – from your child's third birthday till the end of the reception year.

Foundation subject Subjects (other than core subjects) that schools must teach.

Governor One of the people responsible for the direction a school takes, the way it conducts its affairs and develops its ethos.

Home–School Agreement A contract between the school and parents (or other carers) which sets out the way children are expected to behave, usually including attendance, punctuality, discipline and homework.

Inspector A person appointed and accredited by OFSTED (or sometimes by the Local Education Authority) to examine the way individual schools are performing.

Key Stages The stages into which your child's education is divided (Key Stage 1 is roughly equivalent to Infants; Key Stage 2 to Juniors).

Knowledge In terms of the National Curriculum, knowledge is the information that your child is supposed to learn in each subject – for instance, capital cities, the times table.

LEA Local Education Authority.

Lay inspector or lay member An OFSTED inspector with no previous knowledge of teaching or the management of schools; every OFSTED inspection team must have a lay member.

Level (in National Curriculum) A measure of how well your child is doing in the National Curriculum. By the end of Key Stage 2, most children should have attained Level 4.

Literacy Hour An hour a day set aside for children to work on reading and writing.

National Curriculum A framework for schools setting out the knowledge, skills and understanding your child is supposed to learn at various times; it also contains guidance for schools on developing a good ethos.

National league tables or national performance tables Tables showing how children performed in the SATs at schools across the country. Individual children are not named.

National Tests The part of the Standard Assessment Tests that are sent away for independent marking.

Non-statutory framework Guidance for schools in subjects and areas, such as religious education and personal, social and health education, which are in the National Curriculum but which are neither core nor foundation subjects.

Numeracy Hour A time each day set aside for work on mathematics.

OFSTED A government body – the Office for Standards in Education.

Parent–Teacher Association A group within a school set up to ensure good communication between the parents and staff; it may be more or less formal, and may help with things like fundraising.

Registered Inspector The leader of a team of OFSTED inspectors.

SATs Standard Assessment Tests – the tests given at various times in your child's education so teachers can see how the children are doing, and also so they can improve their own performance. These are the basis for the National League Tables.

Scheme of Work Detailed information for teachers, setting out what must be taught at each Key Stage in every subject of the National Curriculum.

Special Educational Needs (SEN) Educational needs that can't be met in the normal course of schooling; they usually refer to children who need extra support because they aren't coping as well as they might, though in theory it could apply to gifted children who need more than the school can provide.

SEN Co-ordinator A teacher responsible for co-ordinating a school's Special Educational Needs provision.

SEN Register An official list of children with Special Educational Needs.

SEN Tribunal An appeal body relating to the placement of children on the SEN Register.

Severe Learning Difficulties Specific problems such as autism or physical disabilities that may affect a child's education.

Skills In terms of the National Curriculum, the ability to carry out specific tasks in different subjects (for example, adding up, using a weighing scale, tying shoe laces).

Special measures Measures set out in response to an OFSTED inspection to help bring a school that is failing back up to standard.

Special school A school for children with Special Educational Needs or Severe Learning Difficulties.

Statement An official document setting out a child's Special Educational Needs with a view to making sure they get the help needed.

Study skills Skills that your child needs in order to be able to learn effectively, such as the ability to organise their workspace and take notes.

Teacher assessment The part of the SATs that is marked by your child's teacher instead of being sent away to independent assessors.

Understanding In terms of the National Curriculum, having a grasp of the basic concepts underlying the knowledge and skills being taught (for instance, understanding that things can be classified according to whether they are alive, dead, or never-alive; or that plants and animals are alive, and that there are basic similarities and differences between them.

Web directory

www.5minutesaway.co.uk 5 minutesaway
www.aardman.com Aardman Animations
www.allgood.demon.co.uk/Default1.htm Horse racing events
www.allmixedup.com All Mixed Up
www.altavista.co.uk Search engine
www.americalinksup.org/planyourown/intterms.html
   Glossary of internet terms
www.angelfire.com/wv/wetzel/index5.html Links to ADHD
   information and resources
www.anglia.co.uk/education/mathsnet Maths Net
www.ask.co.uk Search engine
www.asthma.org.uk National Asthma Campaign
www.atlapedia.com Atalpedia
http://atschool.eduweb.co.uk/ufa10/num_cent.htm Maths
   resources, puzzles and game
www.autism-initiatives.co.uk Autism Initiatives
www.baha.org.uk/ British Activity Holiday Association
www.bbc.co.uk BBC
www.behaviour.org.uk Behavioural problems in children
www.boarding.org.uk/home.htm Boarding Education Alliance
www.bonus.com Bonus.com
www.booktrust.org.uk Book Trust
www.britishcheloniagroup.org.uk The British Chelonia Group
www.budgerigarsociety.com Budgerigar Society
www.bullying.co.uk Bullying
www.cafamily.org.uk Contact a Family
www.camping.org.uk Camping
www.cartooncorner.com Cartoon Corner
www.cats.org.uk Cats Protection League
www.charity-commission.gov.uk/cc49.htm The Charity
   Commission
www.childline.org.uk ChildLine

www.childnet-int.org Childnet International

www.childrenspartnership.org Background reading on internet safety issues

www.choiceineducation.co.uk Choice in Education magazine

www.christmas.com Christmas

www.christmas-time.com Christmas time and carols

www.citizen.org.uk Institute for Citizenship

www.cobisec.org Council of British Independent Schools in the European Communities

www.cookingwithkids.com Cooking with Kids

www.cosmic.org.uk/ptadevon/helpptas.htm#funds Fundraising for parent–teacher associations

www.cyberpatrol.com Internet tools

www.darch.co.uk Boarding schools

www.dfee.gov.uk Department for Education and Employment

www.disney.co.uk Disney UK

http://disney.go.com/legal/internet_safety.html Disney's online internet safety tips

www.dogshome.org Battersea Dogs' Home

www.downscity.com American site providing a forum for the Down syndrome community

www.downsnet.org/downsed The Down Syndrome Educational Trust

www.drw.org.uk Parents divorcing or separating

http://dspace.dial.pipex.com/mcinroy/directory.htm Pub quizzes etc.

www.dyslexia.uk.com British Dyslexics

www.earlybirdsmusic.com Early Birds Music

www.ecd-online.co.uk/sections/support.htm Schools information

www.ed.gov/pubs/parents/internet US government department of education

www.educate.co.uk Educate OnLine

www.educate.org.uk/numeracy.htm Numeracy Hour links

www.education-otherwise.org Education Otherwise

www.eig.org.uk/fws Fireworks code sponsored by Black Cat Fireworks

www.eggsedu.org.uk British Eggs

www.emmbrook.demon.co.uk/dysprax/homepage.htm Dyspraxia

www.english-heritage.org.uk English Heritage
www.english.sports.gov.uk English Sports Council
www.en.eun.org European Schoolnet
www.eurostar.co.uk Eurostar
www.eurotunnel.co.uk Eurotunnel
www.eventselector.co.uk Eventselector
www.ex.ac.uk/bugclub The Bug Club
www.excite.com Search engine
www.explorescience.com Explore Science
www.farm-holidays.co.uk Farm Holidays
www.fire.org.uk/firework/home.htm Official fire service site
www.football365.com Football365
www.forteinc.com Free off-line news readed
www.freeweb.pdg.net/headstrong Museum of home-science
  experiments
www.fundraising.co.uk UK fundraising
www.funfair.ndirect.co.uk/links.html Bouncy castle hire, etc.
www.gdst.net Girls' Day School Trust
www.geocities.com/Athens/Academy/4800 Origami
www.getnetwise.org Online resource for families looking for advice
  on internet safety
**www.go.com/WebDir/Family/Parents_Pages/Internet_issues/I
nternet_content_filters** Links to other sites concerned with
  internet safety issues
www.google.com Search engine
www.greenfingers.com Greenfingers
www.guides.org.uk The Guide Association
www.hamsters.co.uk Complete Hamster Site
www.happychild.org.uk Project HappyChild
www.heas.org.uk Home Education Advisory Service
www.hinchbk.cambs.sch.uk/feast/feasthome.html Organising
  feasts
www.holidays.net/easter Easter
www.home-education.org.uk Home education
http://homepages.tesco.net/~littlebears Home schooling
www.homeworkhigh.com Homework High
www.houserabbit.co.uk British House Rabbit Association
www.howstuffworks.com How Stuff Works
www.iaps.org.uk/iapshome.htm Incorporated Association of
  Preparatory Schools

www.icom.org/vlmp WWW Virtual library

www.icra.org Independent site rating scheme

www.inflatable.co.uk/direct.html Bouncy castle hire, etc

www.infoseek.co.uk Search engine

www.isis.org.uk Independent Schools Information Service

www.iwf.org.uk/ Internet Watch Foundation

www.kidsjokes.co.uk Kids Jokes

www.kidsmusic.co.uk KidsMusic

www.launchsite.org Children's resources

www.learnfree.co.uk Learnfree

www.leisure-hire.co.uk/entertainment.htm Bouncy castle hire, etc.

www.leisurehunt.com LeisureHunt

www.linguanet.org.uk Linguanet

www.literacyhour.co.uk Literacy Hour

www.london.sja.org.uk/sites.htm London St John Ambulance

www.lovelife.hea.org.uk LoveLife

www.mathgoodies.com Math Goodies

www.mathsphere.co.uk MathSphere

www.mathsyear2000.org Maths Year 2000

www.mayhem.org.uk Events

www.mcafee.com Internet tools

www.mclean1953.freeserve.co.uk Child dental care

www.meningitis-trust.org.uk National Meningitis Trust

www.microsys.com/plain_hm.htm Internet tools

www.miju.demon.co.uk Noisey Guinea Pigs

www.moriarty.co.uk Murder-mystery events

www.mp3.com Free songs for download

www.mp3now.com/html/mp3_search.html Top 30 MP3 search engines

www.mp3yes.com MP3 news, downloads, freebies, beginners' guide etc.

www.multimap.com Multimap

www.nafcon.dircon.co.uk/index.html Cyberlizard's

www.nationalgeographic.com National Geographic

www. naturenet.net Naturenet

www.nc.uk.net National Curriculum

www.ncf.org.uk/infoserv.htm National Coaching Foundation

www.nchafc.org.uk NCH Action for Children

www.ncpta.org.uk NCPTA

www.ndcs.org.uk National Deaf Children's Society
www.neige.freeserve.co.uk Charity work and fundraising
www.netdoctor.co.uk Netdoctor
www.netnanny.com Internet tools
www.nfu.org.uk/nafs National Farmers' Union
www.nfucountryside.org.uk National Farmers' Union
www.ngfl.gov.uk National Grid for Learning
www.nhm.ac.uk Natural History Museum
www.nhsdirect.nhs.uk NHS Direct
www.nmsi.ac.uk Science Museum
www.nspcc.org.uk NSPCC
www.odeon.co.uk Odeon Cinemas
www.ofsted.gov.uk OFSTED
www.oneworld.org/autism_uk National Autistic Society
www.onlineweather.com OnlineWeather
http://oposite.stsci.edu/pubinfo/pictures.html Hubble Space
   Telescope
www.pacificnet.net/~johnr/aesop Aesop's Fables
www.paperairplanes.co.uk Paper Airplanes
www.parents.dfee.gov.uk Parents' Centre
www.parents.org.uk Parents Online
www.parents-news.co.uk Schools news
www.patient.org.uk Patient UK
www.pethealthcouncil.co.uk Pet Health Council
www.petstation.com Pet Station
www.pin.org.uk Parents Information Network
www.pony-club.org.uk Pony Club
www.poptel.org.uk/woodcraft Woodcraft Folk
www.primaryresources.co.uk Primary resources
www.pro.gov.uk/education/primary.htm Public Record Office
www.purina.com Choosing a dog questionnaire
www.quite.co.uk/rats Pet rat information
www.real.com Real video
www.recommended-cottages.co.uk Recommended Cottages
www.recycle.mcmail.com/cans.htm Aluminium recycling
www.rnib.org.uk Royal National Institute for the Blind
www.rnid.org.uk Royal National Institute for Deaf People
www.rspb.org.uk Royal Society for the Protection of Birds
www.safekids.com/search.htm Search engine
www.scoot.co.uk Directory of libraries
www.scoutnet.org.uk or **www.scoutbase.org.uk** The Scouts
   Association

www.scran.ac.uk SCRAN
www.shockwave.com Shockwave
www.sportscouncil-ni.org.uk Northern Ireland Sports Council
www.ssc.org.uk Scottish Sports Council
www.st-john-ambulance.org.uk St John Ambulance
www.stageregister.com Guide to drama schools
www.stammering.org British Stammering Association
www.storiestogrowby.com Children's stories
www.teachingideas.co.uk Teaching Ideas
www.tesco.co.uk/information/computers for schools/
   school.htm Tesco computers for school
www.tentaprises.co.uk Marquee hire
www.thames-water.com/watercounts Water Counts
www.theatremuseum.org Theatre Museum
www.theparrotsocietyuk.org The Parrot Society
www.thewarren.demon.co.uk Links to rabbit associations
www.thursdaysclassroom.com Thursday's Classroom
www.tlgleisure.co.uk/castles_1.htm Bouncy castles, etc.
www.topmarks.co.uk Topmarks
www.tortoisetrust.org The Tortoise Trust
www.tradingstandards.gov.uk/schools Trading standards
www.trashed.co.uk Trashed
www.tunes.com Multimedia assets and artist information
www.typographica.com/alice Alice's Adventures in Wonderland
www.uci-cinemas.co.uk UCI Cinemas
www.ukpet.rabbits.org.uk UK pet rabbit community
www.uksport.gov.uk UK Sports Council
www.uktheguide.com UK Guide
www.unclebrian.co.uk Entertainment and event management
www.virgin.net/cinema Virgin Cinemas
www.visitbritain.com Visit Britain
www.web.ukonline.co.uk/conker/fossils Fossil hunting
www.welcome.to/schoolhouse Home education in Scotland
www.weshome.demon.co.uk/teach.html WES Home School
www.wsf.org.uk Women's Sports Foundation
www.yahoo.co.uk Search engine
www.yell.co.uk Directory of libraries

Index

● ● ● ●